Self-Sovereign and Decentralized Identity: The Future of Identity Management

James Relington

DEDICATION

To all cybersecurity professionals. Your commitment to protecting access, enforcing governance, and navigating the complexities of identity management is invaluable. May this work serve as a guide and inspiration in your ongoing efforts to create a more secure and compliant future.

AKNOWLEDGEMENTS

I extend my deepest gratitude to everyone who contributed to the creation of this book. To my colleagues and mentors in the field of identity governance, your insights and expertise have been invaluable. To my friends and family, your unwavering support and encouragement have made this journey possible. To the professionals and innovators dedicated to securing digital identities, your work continues to inspire and shape the future of cybersecurity. This book is a reflection of collective knowledge, and I am grateful to all who have played a role in its development.

The Evolution of Identity Management

Identity management has undergone a significant transformation throughout history, adapting to societal changes, technological advancements, and the increasing complexities of digital interactions. In its earliest form, identity was a purely physical concept, tied to face-to-face recognition within small communities. Individuals were identified by their names, lineage, or personal attributes, and trust was built through direct social interactions. As societies grew and trade expanded beyond local villages, the need for more formal identity verification methods emerged, leading to the creation of documents such as seals, signatures, and official records maintained by authorities.

With the rise of nation-states and organized governance, identity systems became more structured. Governments introduced birth certificates, national ID cards, and passports to establish official identity records. These systems centralized identity management under state control, allowing for more efficient administration of social services, taxation, and law enforcement. However, they also introduced new challenges, particularly concerning privacy, surveillance, and the exclusion of individuals without proper documentation. Identity was now something assigned and controlled by institutions rather than solely existing as a self-evident trait of an individual.

The digital revolution brought about another seismic shift in identity management. The internet and online services required new ways to verify and authenticate users. Initially, identity in the digital space was informal, with individuals creating usernames and passwords to access websites and services. However, as online interactions became more sophisticated and commerce moved to digital platforms, stronger authentication methods were needed. This led to the development of centralized identity management systems, where companies and institutions stored user credentials, allowing individuals to log in using an email address or social media account.

While centralized identity systems offered convenience, they also introduced significant risks. The concentration of sensitive user data in the hands of a few organizations made these entities prime targets for cyberattacks. Data breaches exposed millions of users to identity theft, fraud, and privacy violations. Additionally, centralized models raised concerns over control and autonomy. Companies like Facebook, Google, and Apple became gatekeepers of digital identity, dictating access to various online services. Users were no longer in full control of their personal information, as corporations harvested and monetized data without meaningful user consent.

The emergence of federated identity management sought to address some of these issues by allowing users to authenticate across multiple services using a single identity provider. Single sign-on (SSO) solutions, such as those provided by Google or Microsoft, reduced the need for multiple passwords and improved user experience. However, these solutions still relied on centralized entities, perpetuating the same concerns of data control, surveillance, and vulnerability to breaches. While federated identity improved convenience, it did not fundamentally alter the power dynamics of identity ownership.

As concerns over privacy, security, and digital sovereignty grew, decentralized identity management emerged as a compelling alternative. The development of blockchain technology and cryptographic advancements enabled new identity paradigms that prioritize user control and self-sovereignty. Unlike traditional systems, decentralized identity shifts power from centralized authorities to individuals, allowing them to own and manage their identity without relying on intermediaries. With the introduction of decentralized identifiers (DIDs) and verifiable credentials, users can prove their identity without exposing unnecessary personal information. This approach enhances privacy, reduces reliance on centralized databases, and mitigates the risks associated with large-scale data breaches.

Governments, organizations, and technology developers are now exploring self-sovereign identity (SSI) solutions as a means to improve identity security while granting individuals greater control over their personal data. SSI frameworks enable users to store their identity credentials in digital wallets, selectively disclosing information as needed. For example, a person could prove their age without revealing their full date of birth, minimizing the exposure of sensitive information. This selective disclosure enhances privacy while maintaining trust between individuals and service providers.

Despite the promise of decentralized identity, challenges remain. Adoption barriers, interoperability concerns, and regulatory uncertainties present significant hurdles to widespread implementation. Governments and institutions accustomed to centralized control may resist shifting to decentralized models, fearing loss of oversight and potential misuse of self-managed identities. Additionally, user experience remains a critical factor in adoption; for decentralized identity to succeed, it must be as seamless and intuitive as traditional authentication methods.

The evolution of identity management reflects the broader technological and societal shifts that have shaped human interactions over centuries. From tribal recognition to government-issued documents, from centralized databases to decentralized frameworks, identity management continues to evolve in response to the changing needs of individuals and institutions. As new technologies emerge and the demand for privacy grows, the future of identity is likely to be defined by a balance between security, convenience, and user empowerment. The transition from centralized to self-sovereign identity represents not just a technological advancement but a fundamental shift in how individuals assert and control their own identities in the digital age.

Centralized vs. Decentralized Identity Systems

Identity systems have traditionally been centralized, with governments, corporations, and institutions acting as the primary authorities responsible for verifying and managing personal identities. These systems have provided the backbone for modern economies, enabling individuals to access financial services, healthcare, education, and other essential resources. However, the centralized nature of these identity systems has also introduced numerous vulnerabilities, including privacy risks, data breaches, and excessive control by third-party entities. As digital interactions have become more frequent and globalized, the limitations of centralized identity management have become increasingly evident, paving the way for the rise of decentralized identity systems.

Centralized identity systems operate under a model where a single entity, such as a government, bank, or technology company, is responsible for issuing and verifying identities. In this framework, individuals must rely on third parties to validate their credentials, whether in the form of passports, driver's licenses, social security numbers, or login credentials for online services. While this approach has provided efficiency and standardization, it has also created a system in which users have limited control over their personal data. Institutions that store and manage identities become central points of failure, meaning that if a system is compromised, millions of identities can be exposed or manipulated.

A major drawback of centralized identity systems is the risk of data breaches. Large-scale hacks have demonstrated the vulnerability of centralized databases, with incidents affecting companies such as Equifax, Facebook, and government agencies worldwide. When a single organization holds vast amounts of sensitive user data, it becomes an attractive target for cybercriminals. The consequences of these breaches are severe, leading to identity theft, financial fraud, and loss of personal privacy. Furthermore, centralized systems often require users to share more information than necessary, increasing the risk of personal data being misused or exploited for commercial purposes.

Another issue with centralized identity systems is the dependence on intermediaries. Users must trust organizations to store and protect their information while also relying on them for authentication and access to services. This reliance not only places power in the hands of corporations and governments but also creates a system where users have little to no agency over how their identity is managed. Additionally, centralized identity models can be exclusionary, as individuals without official government-issued documents or access to traditional financial institutions may struggle to prove their identity and participate fully in the digital economy.

In contrast, decentralized identity systems seek to eliminate reliance on central authorities by enabling individuals to control and manage their own identities. This approach is made possible through cryptographic technologies, blockchain, and decentralized identifiers (DIDs), allowing users to create and own their digital identity without the need for intermediaries. Instead of storing identity data in a single centralized database, decentralized systems distribute control across multiple nodes, reducing the risks associated with data breaches and unauthorized access.

One of the key benefits of decentralized identity is enhanced privacy and security. With this model, users can selectively disclose only the necessary information for verification, rather than handing over extensive personal data to a third party. For example, instead of sharing a full government-issued ID to verify age, a decentralized identity system would allow a user to prove they are above a certain age without revealing their date of birth. This minimizes exposure and mitigates the risk of personal information being stored, shared, or sold without consent.

Self-sovereign identity (SSI) is a critical concept within decentralized identity systems. It emphasizes the idea that individuals should have full ownership and control over their identity, rather than relying on institutions to issue or manage it. In an SSI framework, users store their identity credentials in a digital wallet, issuing verifiable proofs as needed. These credentials can be authenticated through decentralized networks, ensuring that trust is established without dependence on a central authority. This approach shifts the power dynamic, giving individuals greater autonomy while also improving security and reducing the impact of data breaches.

Despite the advantages of decentralized identity, there are still challenges to widespread adoption. One of the biggest hurdles is interoperability—ensuring that decentralized identity solutions work seamlessly across different platforms, industries, and jurisdictions. While decentralized identifiers and verifiable credentials are gaining traction, standardization remains an ongoing process. Many organizations and governments are hesitant to transition from centralized models, given their existing infrastructure and regulatory frameworks. Additionally, decentralized identity systems require a level of digital literacy that may not be accessible to all users, creating potential barriers to adoption.

Another challenge is the issue of identity recovery. In centralized systems, lost passwords or compromised accounts can be restored through established recovery mechanisms such as email verification or customer support. In a decentralized identity system, however, users bear the responsibility of managing their own private keys. If a private key is lost or stolen, recovering an identity can be complex, requiring multi-party verification or social recovery methods. Solutions are being developed to address this issue, but ensuring both security and usability remains a delicate balance.

Despite these challenges, decentralized identity represents a paradigm shift that aligns with the broader movement toward privacy, security, and user empowerment in the digital age. The transition from centralized to decentralized identity is not merely a technological change but a fundamental rethinking of how identity is owned, verified, and used. As blockchain and cryptographic innovations continue to evolve, decentralized identity systems have the potential to provide a more secure, inclusive, and privacy-preserving framework for identity management, giving individuals control over their own digital identities in a way that centralized models never could.

The Principles of Self-Sovereign Identity (SSI)

Self-sovereign identity (SSI) represents a paradigm shift in how individuals manage and control their digital identities. Unlike traditional identity models, which rely on centralized authorities such as governments, corporations, and institutions, SSI places identity ownership directly in the hands of individuals. This approach is built on principles that emphasize user autonomy, privacy, security, and interoperability, creating a foundation for a more decentralized and user-centric identity ecosystem. As digital interactions become increasingly prevalent, the need for a secure and privacy-respecting identity framework has never been greater. SSI seeks to address this need by fundamentally rethinking the way identity is created, stored, shared, and verified.

A core principle of self-sovereign identity is individual ownership and control. In conventional identity systems, users must rely on external entities to issue and verify their credentials, often without having full access to or control over their personal data. This creates a system where users are dependent on intermediaries, and their identities can be revoked or misused without their consent. SSI removes this dependency by allowing individuals to generate and manage their own digital identities, ensuring that they have full authority over how and when their credentials are shared. This shift from institutional control to personal ownership redefines the power dynamics of identity management.

Privacy is another fundamental principle of SSI. Traditional identity models often require users to disclose excessive amounts of personal information to access services, leading to unnecessary data collection and storage by third parties. These centralized databases become attractive targets for hackers, increasing the risk of identity theft and fraud. SSI mitigates this risk by enabling selective disclosure, allowing users to share only the specific pieces of information required for a given transaction. For instance, instead of presenting an entire driver's license to verify age, a user can cryptographically prove they are over a certain age without revealing their date of birth or other sensitive details. This concept, often facilitated by zero-knowledge proofs, enhances privacy while maintaining trust between users and service providers.

Security is a crucial aspect of self-sovereign identity. Traditional identity systems store user credentials in centralized repositories, making them vulnerable to breaches, data leaks, and unauthorized access. In contrast, SSI leverages cryptographic techniques and decentralized technologies such as blockchain to enhance security. Instead of storing identity data on a central server, SSI enables users to store their credentials in secure digital wallets. These wallets allow users to manage their credentials independently while maintaining verifiable proof of authenticity. Public-key cryptography ensures that only the rightful owner can control and use their identity, significantly reducing the risk of impersonation or data breaches.

Interoperability is another key principle that ensures the widespread adoption and usability of self-sovereign identity. Identity should not be confined to specific platforms, organizations, or jurisdictions; instead, users should be able to use their digital credentials seamlessly across different services and environments. SSI frameworks promote open standards, such as decentralized identifiers (DIDs) and verifiable credentials, to enable compatibility between various identity systems. This ensures that an identity issued in one ecosystem can be recognized and verified in another, promoting a more interconnected and user-friendly identity infrastructure.

Decentralization plays a vital role in ensuring that self-sovereign identity is not controlled by any single entity. Traditional identity systems often suffer from single points of failure, where a breach or policy change can have widespread consequences for users. SSI eliminates these vulnerabilities by distributing trust across a decentralized network. Blockchain and distributed ledger technologies provide a way to verify identity credentials without relying on a central authority. This ensures that no single entity has control over the identity ecosystem, reducing the risk of censorship, manipulation, or misuse of personal data.

Another important principle of SSI is user consent and transparency. In centralized identity models, users often have little visibility into how their data is collected, stored, and shared. Many organizations monetize user data without explicit consent, leading to ethical and legal concerns. SSI addresses this issue by ensuring that users have complete control over when and how their credentials are shared. Transactions involving identity verification are transparent and require explicit user approval, eliminating the hidden data exchanges that are common in traditional systems. This fosters greater trust between individuals and service providers, as users can be confident that their data is not being exploited.

Persistence is also a crucial consideration in self-sovereign identity. An individual's identity should not be tied to a specific provider that could revoke access or disappear entirely. Unlike social media accounts or email-based logins that can be terminated at the discretion of a company, SSI ensures that users retain access to their identities indefinitely. The use of decentralized identifiers and blockchain-based registries ensures that identity credentials remain verifiable and accessible regardless of changes in organizational policies or technological shifts. This persistence is especially important for individuals in vulnerable situations, such as refugees or those without access to government-issued documents, who need a reliable way to prove their identity over time.

Portability is another significant advantage of SSI. Users should not be locked into a single platform or system but should instead have the ability to use their identity credentials across multiple services and jurisdictions. Traditional identity models often require users to create separate credentials for different organizations, leading to fragmentation and inconvenience. With SSI, individuals can carry their digital identities with them, using the same verifiable credentials for financial services, healthcare, education, and other interactions. This portability reduces redundancy and streamlines the identity verification process while maintaining user autonomy.

Equity and inclusion are also important aspects of self-sovereign identity. Many people around the world lack formal identity documentation, preventing them from accessing essential services such as banking, healthcare, and education. Traditional identity systems can be exclusionary, particularly for marginalized populations who may not have government-issued IDs or who live in regions with weak institutional infrastructure. SSI provides a more inclusive solution by allowing individuals to create and manage their own digital identities, independent of state control. By enabling identity verification through decentralized networks, SSI opens up new opportunities for people who have historically been excluded from formal identity systems.

The shift toward self-sovereign identity represents a fundamental rethinking of how identity is managed in the digital age. By prioritizing user ownership, privacy, security, and interoperability, SSI offers a more equitable and resilient approach to identity management. The adoption of these principles has the potential to reshape digital interactions, creating a future where individuals have full control over their personal data and can interact with digital services on their own terms. As technology and regulations evolve, the principles of SSI will continue to guide the development of identity systems that empower users while ensuring security and trust in an increasingly digital world.

Trust Models in Identity Systems

Trust is the foundation of any identity system, determining how individuals, organizations, and systems authenticate and verify identities. Without trust, interactions in both physical and digital environments become inefficient, insecure, and unreliable. Trust models in identity systems define the mechanisms by which entities establish confidence in the authenticity of credentials and claims. These models have evolved from centralized, institution-driven frameworks to more decentralized and self-sovereign approaches, reflecting the changing dynamics of identity ownership, security, and verification in the digital age.

Traditional identity systems operate on a centralized trust model, where a single authoritative entity acts as the ultimate source of truth. Governments, banks, universities, and large corporations serve as identity providers, issuing and verifying credentials such as passports, driver's licenses, bank accounts, and diplomas. In this model, trust is placed in a central authority that validates an individual's identity based on predefined policies and regulations. While this approach provides consistency and widespread recognition, it also creates single points of failure. If the issuing authority is compromised, either through data breaches, corruption, or system failures, the entire trust structure collapses, exposing users to fraud and identity theft.

A federated trust model emerged as an evolution of the centralized system, allowing multiple identity providers to share authentication responsibilities. This model is commonly used in single sign-on (SSO) solutions, where users can access multiple services using a single set of credentials. Organizations such as Google, Facebook, and Microsoft act as identity providers, enabling users to log into third-party applications without creating new accounts. Federated identity models improve convenience and reduce the burden of managing multiple credentials, but they still rely on a small number of powerful entities. Users must trust these providers to manage their identity securely, and any breach or misuse of data at the provider level affects all services that depend on that identity.

The decentralized trust model aims to shift control away from central authorities, allowing trust to be distributed among multiple participants. Instead of relying on a single entity to verify identities, decentralized identity systems use cryptographic techniques, blockchain technology, and peer-to-peer networks to establish trust. Self-sovereign identity (SSI) is a key example of this model, where individuals control their own identity credentials and present verifiable proofs without depending on intermediaries. In this framework, trust is established through cryptographic verification rather than institutional authority, enabling users to share only the necessary information while maintaining privacy and security.

Blockchain technology has played a crucial role in enabling decentralized trust models. By creating an immutable ledger of transactions and credentials, blockchain ensures that identity claims cannot be tampered with or altered. In a decentralized identity system, credentials issued by trusted entities, such as universities or employers, are recorded on a distributed ledger. Users store these credentials in their digital wallets and present them when needed, with service providers verifying their authenticity through blockchain records. This eliminates the need for a central authority to validate claims, reducing dependency on single points of failure and enhancing security.

Trust in identity systems also relies on verification mechanisms that ensure the legitimacy of credentials. In centralized and federated models, verification is performed by the issuing authority or an authorized third party. For example, when a bank verifies a customer's identity, it cross-checks information with government-issued records. In decentralized models, verification is done through cryptographic proofs, allowing entities to confirm the authenticity of a claim without accessing the underlying personal data. Zero-knowledge proofs, a key innovation in privacy-preserving identity verification, enable individuals to prove facts about their identity—such as being over 18 or possessing a valid degree—without disclosing additional details.

Another dimension of trust in identity systems is the reputation-based model, where trust is built through accumulated verifications and interactions. Online marketplaces, professional networks, and social platforms often use reputation scores, endorsements, and transaction histories to establish credibility. While this model offers a more dynamic and user-driven approach to trust, it also introduces risks related to manipulation, bias, and the potential for exclusion based on subjective criteria. Decentralized identity systems can integrate reputation mechanisms using verifiable credentials, ensuring that trust is built on objective, tamper-proof records rather than centralized ratings.

The role of governance in trust models is also significant. Identity systems must balance security, privacy, and compliance with regulatory requirements. Governments and regulatory bodies set standards for identity verification, fraud prevention, and anti-money laundering (AML) measures, shaping how trust is established in digital identity ecosystems. Decentralized identity models challenge traditional governance structures by reducing reliance on centralized authorities, prompting discussions on how regulatory frameworks can adapt to new trust paradigms. Some governments have begun exploring blockchain-based identity solutions, integrating decentralized verification while maintaining oversight and compliance mechanisms.

User trust in identity systems is influenced by factors beyond technology, including transparency, ease of use, and control over personal data. Centralized models have often been criticized for their lack of transparency, where users are unaware of how their data is stored, shared, or monetized. Decentralized identity systems aim to address these concerns by providing users with clear visibility into how their credentials are managed and allowing them to revoke access when needed. However, for decentralized trust models to gain widespread adoption, they must also be user-friendly and intuitive. If identity management becomes too complex, users may revert to familiar centralized solutions, even if they are less secure or privacy-preserving.

The evolution of trust models in identity systems reflects a broader shift toward decentralization, privacy, and user empowerment. While centralized models continue to dominate due to their established infrastructure and regulatory acceptance, decentralized identity solutions are gaining traction as technology advances and concerns over data security grow. The future of trust in identity management will likely involve a hybrid approach, where decentralized verification methods complement existing centralized frameworks, providing a more resilient and privacy-conscious identity ecosystem. As trust models continue to evolve, the balance between security, usability, and autonomy will define the next generation of identity systems.

Digital Identity and Privacy Considerations

Digital identity has become an essential part of modern life, enabling individuals to access online services, verify their credentials, and interact with institutions across the globe. From banking and healthcare to social media and e-commerce, digital identity plays a crucial role in both personal and professional interactions. However, as digital identity systems become more widespread, they also raise significant concerns regarding privacy, data security, and individual autonomy. The way digital identities are managed and shared determines not only convenience and security but also the level of control that users have over their personal information.

Traditional digital identity systems often rely on centralized authorities, such as governments, banks, or technology companies, to issue and verify credentials. These centralized systems collect and store vast amounts of personal data, creating risks related to data breaches, identity theft, and unauthorized access. Once an individual's data is stored in a central database, they have little control over how it is used, who can access it, or whether it is shared with third parties. Many organizations monetize personal data without user consent, turning identity information into a commodity that fuels targeted advertising and other commercial activities.

The rise of social media and single sign-on (SSO) solutions has further complicated digital identity privacy. Platforms such as Facebook, Google, and Apple allow users to log into multiple services using a single identity, streamlining access but also consolidating control under a few powerful entities. While these systems offer convenience, they also create privacy risks by enabling extensive tracking of user activity across different applications and websites. Personal information, browsing habits, and behavioral data are collected, analyzed, and stored indefinitely, often without clear transparency regarding how this data is used or shared.

One of the main privacy concerns in digital identity systems is the risk of data breaches. Centralized identity repositories have become prime targets for cybercriminals, leading to massive data leaks that expose sensitive information. Stolen digital identities can be used for fraud, impersonation, and financial crimes, causing long-term harm to affected individuals. Once personal data is compromised, it is nearly impossible to regain control over its distribution, as leaked information can be sold on the dark web and misused indefinitely. The lack of user control over stored identity information makes traditional identity systems inherently vulnerable to large-scale security incidents.

Decentralized identity models have emerged as a response to these privacy concerns, shifting control away from centralized authorities and placing it directly in the hands of users. Self-sovereign identity (SSI) allows individuals to create and manage their digital identities independently, using blockchain technology and cryptographic methods to verify credentials without relying on third parties. Instead of storing identity data in centralized databases, users keep their credentials in secure digital wallets, choosing when and how to share their information. This approach enhances privacy by minimizing unnecessary data collection and reducing exposure to cyber threats.

Selective disclosure is a critical feature of privacy-preserving digital identity systems. Instead of sharing an entire identity document, individuals can provide only the specific information required for verification. For example, to confirm eligibility for a service that requires users to be over 18, an SSI system would allow a user to prove their age without revealing their full date of birth. Zero-knowledge proofs and cryptographic attestations enable this level of privacy protection, ensuring that sensitive details remain undisclosed while still satisfying verification requirements. This method significantly reduces the amount of personal data exposed to third parties, lowering the risk of misuse and surveillance.

Government initiatives and regulatory frameworks have attempted to address privacy issues in digital identity management, but their effectiveness varies widely. Regulations such as the General Data Protection Regulation (GDPR) in Europe have introduced stricter data protection measures, requiring organizations to obtain explicit user consent before collecting or processing personal data. GDPR also grants individuals the right to access, correct, and delete their personal information, reinforcing the principle of user control. However, enforcement challenges and loopholes in regulatory frameworks often leave individuals vulnerable to data exploitation, especially when dealing with multinational corporations that operate across different jurisdictions.

Biometric identity systems present additional privacy challenges, as they rely on unique physical characteristics such as fingerprints, facial recognition, and iris scans for authentication. While biometrics offer a high level of security, they also raise concerns about surveillance, data permanence, and potential misuse by governments or corporations. Unlike passwords, biometric data cannot be changed if compromised, making breaches particularly damaging. Additionally, widespread adoption of biometric authentication has led to concerns about mass surveillance, where governments and private entities can track individuals without their knowledge or consent. The increasing use of facial recognition technology in public spaces has sparked debates about the balance between security and civil liberties.

Privacy risks in digital identity systems are also influenced by emerging technologies such as artificial intelligence (AI) and big data analytics. AI-driven identity verification and behavioral tracking enable more accurate fraud detection and security monitoring but also introduce risks related to bias, discrimination, and ethical concerns. Machine learning algorithms trained on biased datasets can reinforce existing inequalities, leading to unfair treatment in areas such as hiring, credit scoring, and law enforcement. Additionally, AI-powered identity systems can be exploited for invasive surveillance, as governments and corporations use predictive analytics to monitor and control populations.

The future of digital identity privacy depends on the development of technologies and policies that prioritize user control, security, and transparency. Privacy-enhancing technologies such as decentralized identifiers (DIDs), verifiable credentials, and confidential computing offer promising solutions for protecting personal data while enabling secure digital interactions. Decentralized identity networks, supported by open standards and interoperable protocols, can provide a viable alternative to traditional centralized models, reducing reliance on intermediaries and strengthening user autonomy.

Education and awareness also play a crucial role in improving digital identity privacy. Many users are unaware of how their personal data is collected, shared, and monetized by online platforms and service providers. Increasing public understanding of privacy risks, encryption technologies, and digital rights can empower individuals to make informed choices about their online identity management. Organizations and governments must also take responsibility for implementing ethical and transparent identity policies that prioritize individual privacy over profit-driven data exploitation.

Striking a balance between security, usability, and privacy is essential for the future of digital identity. While strong authentication and identity verification are necessary for preventing fraud and ensuring trust, they must not come at the cost of personal privacy. Digital identity systems should be designed with built-in privacy safeguards, minimizing data exposure and giving individuals full control over their personal information. As new identity solutions emerge, the challenge lies in creating a digital identity landscape that is both secure and respectful of user privacy, ensuring that individuals can participate in the digital world without compromising their fundamental rights.

Blockchain and Its Role in Decentralized Identity

Blockchain technology has emerged as a foundational component of decentralized identity, offering a secure and tamper-resistant framework for identity management. Traditional identity systems rely on centralized authorities such as governments, corporations, or financial institutions to issue, verify, and store identity credentials. While these models have provided structure and security in the past, they also create single points of failure, expose users to privacy risks, and limit individual control over personal data. Blockchain introduces a decentralized alternative that eliminates the need for intermediaries, allowing individuals to manage their identities in a more secure and autonomous manner.

At its core, blockchain is a distributed ledger technology that records transactions across multiple nodes in a network, ensuring that data remains immutable and transparent. Unlike centralized databases, where a single entity controls and stores information, blockchain distributes data across a decentralized network, making it resistant to tampering and censorship. This decentralized nature is crucial for identity management, as it removes the reliance on a single trusted authority and instead enables a system where multiple parties can verify and authenticate identity claims without compromising security or privacy.

One of the key features of blockchain in decentralized identity is the concept of decentralized identifiers (DIDs). A DID is a unique, blockchain-based identifier that an individual can create and control without requiring permission from a centralized entity. Unlike traditional identifiers such as email addresses or usernames, which are often linked to corporate databases, DIDs are independent and can be used across different platforms and services without reliance on a central authority. This ensures that individuals maintain ownership of their digital identities and are not subject to arbitrary restrictions or revocations imposed by external organizations.

Verifiable credentials (VCs) are another essential component of blockchain-based identity systems. In traditional identity models, credentials such as passports, driver's licenses, or diplomas are issued and stored by central authorities, requiring users to request verification from these entities whenever they need to prove their identity. With blockchain-based verifiable credentials, individuals receive cryptographic proofs of their identity attributes, which they can store in a digital wallet and present whenever needed. These credentials can be verified using blockchain records without the need for direct communication with the issuing authority, streamlining identity verification while enhancing security and privacy.

Privacy is a critical consideration in decentralized identity, and blockchain plays a key role in ensuring that personal data remains protected. Unlike centralized systems that store sensitive information in a single location, blockchain-based identity solutions use cryptographic techniques to enable privacy-preserving identity verification. Zero-knowledge proofs (ZKPs) are one such method, allowing individuals to prove specific claims about their identity without revealing the underlying data. For example, a person could use a ZKP to confirm that they are over 18 years old without disclosing their exact date of birth. This approach minimizes data exposure and reduces the risk of identity theft or misuse.

Security is another major advantage of using blockchain for decentralized identity. Traditional identity systems are vulnerable to hacking, data breaches, and unauthorized access, as they store vast amounts of sensitive information in centralized repositories. Blockchain's decentralized architecture significantly reduces these risks by eliminating single points of failure. Because identity data is not stored directly on the blockchain but rather linked through cryptographic hashes and decentralized identifiers, attackers cannot access or modify user credentials even if they manage to compromise a single node in the network. This distributed security model makes blockchain an ideal solution for identity management in an increasingly digital world.

Interoperability is a challenge in existing identity systems, as different organizations and platforms often use proprietary identity solutions that do not communicate with one another. Blockchain-based identity systems address this issue by supporting open standards for identity verification and authentication. Decentralized identity frameworks built on blockchain, such as those developed by the World Wide Web Consortium (W3C), enable seamless integration across various services and industries. This means that a single digital identity can be used for multiple purposes, from accessing financial services and healthcare records to proving educational qualifications and voting in digital elections.

The role of blockchain in decentralized identity extends beyond individual users to enterprises and governments seeking to implement more secure and transparent identity systems. Governments around the world are exploring blockchain-based digital identity initiatives to improve citizen services, reduce fraud, and enhance trust in public administration. Countries such as Estonia, Canada, and Singapore have piloted blockchain identity programs that allow citizens to access government services using decentralized credentials. These initiatives demonstrate the potential of blockchain to streamline identity verification processes while maintaining privacy and security at scale.

Despite its advantages, blockchain-based identity systems also face challenges that must be addressed for widespread adoption. Scalability remains a concern, as blockchain networks can become slow and inefficient when handling large volumes of transactions. Solutions such as layer 2 scaling technologies and sidechains are being developed to mitigate these issues, ensuring that blockchain identity systems can support global adoption without compromising performance.

Another challenge is regulatory compliance, as governments and institutions must establish clear legal frameworks for recognizing and accepting blockchain-based identity credentials. While decentralized identity offers greater privacy and user control, it also raises concerns about compliance with anti-money laundering (AML) and know-your-customer (KYC) regulations. Governments and regulatory bodies must strike a balance between enabling decentralized identity solutions and ensuring that they meet legal and security requirements.

User experience is another factor that will determine the success of blockchain-based identity solutions. While the technology offers significant security and privacy benefits, it must also be accessible and easy to use for individuals with varying levels of digital literacy. Managing decentralized identifiers, private keys, and verifiable credentials requires a user-friendly interface and clear guidelines to ensure that people can navigate decentralized identity systems without confusion or technical barriers. Efforts are being made to develop intuitive identity wallets and authentication mechanisms that simplify the user experience while maintaining security and decentralization.

The integration of blockchain into identity systems represents a fundamental shift in how identity is managed, verified, and secured in the digital age. By replacing centralized control with decentralized trust, blockchain enables individuals to take ownership of their digital identities while reducing reliance on intermediaries. As technology continues to evolve and regulatory frameworks adapt, blockchain-based decentralized identity has the potential to redefine online authentication, privacy, and security, creating a more inclusive and user-centric digital identity ecosystem.

Verifiable Credentials: Concepts and Applications

Verifiable credentials (VCs) are a core component of decentralized identity systems, enabling individuals and organizations to issue, hold, and verify identity-related claims in a secure and privacy-preserving manner. Unlike traditional identity credentials, which rely on centralized authorities for verification, verifiable credentials leverage cryptographic techniques and decentralized trust frameworks to provide secure, tamper-proof, and easily verifiable digital credentials. These credentials can represent various types of information, such as government-issued IDs, academic degrees, professional certifications, or proof of membership in an organization. By enabling individuals to control their own credentials and share them selectively, verifiable credentials offer a new approach to digital identity that enhances security, privacy, and user autonomy.

A verifiable credential consists of three primary components: the issuer, the holder, and the verifier. The issuer is the entity that creates and signs the credential, such as a university that issues a diploma or a government agency that provides a driver's license. The holder is the individual who owns and stores the credential in a digital wallet, allowing them to present it when needed. The verifier is the entity that requests proof of identity or a specific claim, such as an employer verifying a job candidate's educational background. This model eliminates the need for direct communication between the issuer and verifier, as credentials can be independently verified through cryptographic proofs.

A crucial aspect of verifiable credentials is the use of digital signatures and decentralized identifiers (DIDs) to ensure authenticity and integrity. When an issuer creates a credential, they sign it using their private cryptographic key, generating a tamper-proof proof of issuance. The verifier can then check the signature against the issuer's public key, confirming that the credential is valid and has not been altered. Because this verification process occurs independently of the issuer, it reduces the risk of fraud and removes the need for continuous reliance on centralized authorities. This decentralized approach enhances security and efficiency in identity verification.

One of the key advantages of verifiable credentials is their ability to enable selective disclosure. Traditional identity verification often requires individuals to share excessive amounts of personal information, exposing them to unnecessary privacy risks. For example, when proving age eligibility for a service, individuals typically present a full government-issued ID, revealing sensitive details such as their full name, date of birth, and address. With verifiable credentials, users can disclose only the specific information required, such as proving that they are over 18 without sharing their exact birth date. This is achieved using cryptographic techniques like zero-knowledge proofs, which allow for verification without revealing underlying data.

Verifiable credentials have broad applications across various industries, transforming how identity verification is conducted in digital and physical interactions. In the education sector, universities and certification bodies can issue digital diplomas and professional credentials as verifiable credentials, allowing graduates to share their qualifications with employers, licensing boards, or academic institutions. Instead of relying on traditional paper-based certificates or slow, manual verification processes, employers can instantly verify an applicant's degree through cryptographic proofs, ensuring authenticity and reducing the risk of credential fraud.

In financial services, verifiable credentials play a critical role in streamlining know-your-customer (KYC) and anti-money laundering (AML) compliance. Banks and financial institutions require customers to provide identity documents for account opening and transactions, often leading to cumbersome and repetitive verification procedures. With verifiable credentials, individuals can present cryptographically signed identity proofs without repeatedly sharing sensitive documents. This not only enhances security but also reduces compliance costs and improves the customer experience. By minimizing reliance on centralized databases, financial institutions can lower their exposure to data breaches while maintaining compliance with regulatory requirements.

Healthcare is another domain where verifiable credentials can enhance security, efficiency, and privacy. Patients can receive verifiable credentials for medical records, vaccination certificates, or prescriptions, allowing them to share necessary health information with doctors, hospitals, or insurance providers without exposing unrelated personal data. For example, a patient could present proof of COVID-19 vaccination using a verifiable credential, ensuring that the certificate is authentic without revealing additional health details. This approach improves interoperability between healthcare providers while maintaining strict privacy controls, reducing the risks associated with centralized medical data storage.

Verifiable credentials also offer solutions for government services and e-governance, enabling citizens to access digital public services in a secure and privacy-preserving manner. Government-issued digital identities, residency permits, and social security credentials can be transformed into verifiable credentials, allowing individuals to prove their eligibility for services without unnecessary data exposure. Decentralized identity frameworks built on verifiable credentials can improve voter authentication in digital elections, enhance border control procedures, and streamline interactions between citizens and government agencies. By reducing dependence on centralized identity repositories, governments can strengthen data security and enhance trust in digital public services.

The integration of verifiable credentials into the workforce and professional environments provides significant benefits for hiring, employment verification, and workplace access management. Organizations can issue verifiable credentials for employee IDs, skill certifications, and background checks, allowing for seamless and trustworthy authentication in hiring and internal access control. Instead of relying on third-party background checks, which are often slow and prone to errors, employers can verify a candidate's credentials instantly and securely. This approach reduces hiring fraud, improves onboarding efficiency, and strengthens workplace security.

Despite their advantages, verifiable credentials face challenges in adoption and implementation. One key challenge is the need for global standards and interoperability between different identity systems. While organizations such as the World Wide Web Consortium (W3C) have developed specifications for verifiable credentials, widespread adoption requires cooperation between governments, businesses, and technology providers to ensure seamless cross-platform compatibility. Without standardized frameworks, the risk of fragmentation increases, limiting the effectiveness of verifiable credentials in global identity ecosystems.

Another challenge is the usability and accessibility of verifiable credential solutions. While digital wallets and decentralized identity frameworks offer enhanced security and privacy, they must also be user-friendly and intuitive for individuals with varying levels of digital literacy. Managing cryptographic keys and digital credentials requires a balance between security and ease of use, ensuring that individuals can easily store, retrieve, and share their credentials without technical barriers. Efforts are being made to develop user-friendly identity wallets that simplify credential management while maintaining strong security measures.

As digital identity systems continue to evolve, verifiable credentials are positioned to play a central role in shaping the future of identity management. By providing a secure, privacy-preserving, and interoperable solution for identity verification, verifiable credentials empower individuals with greater control over their personal information while reducing reliance on centralized authorities. The adoption of verifiable credentials across industries has the potential to transform identity verification processes, making them more efficient, secure, and user-centric. As more organizations and governments recognize the benefits of decentralized identity, the use of verifiable credentials will continue to expand, enabling a more secure and privacy-conscious digital world.

Decentralized Identifiers (DIDs): The New Standard

Decentralized Identifiers (DIDs) represent a fundamental shift in how digital identity is managed, moving away from centralized identity systems controlled by governments, corporations, or other intermediaries. Unlike traditional identifiers such as email addresses, social media handles, or government-issued ID numbers, DIDs are self-sovereign, meaning that individuals or organizations create and control them without reliance on a central authority. This new standard provides a decentralized, secure, and privacy-preserving way to authenticate and verify identity across digital and physical interactions. By leveraging blockchain and cryptographic technology, DIDs ensure that users can maintain ownership of their identity while reducing the risks associated with centralized data storage and third-party control.

A DID is a unique string of characters, similar in function to a URL, that points to an identity document containing cryptographic keys, verification methods, and metadata. Unlike traditional identifiers that are issued and managed by centralized entities, DIDs are generated and owned by the user. Each DID is associated with a DID document, which contains information about how the identifier can be verified, such as public keys or service endpoints. These documents are stored on decentralized networks, ensuring that identity records remain tamper-proof and accessible without the need for a central authority.

One of the primary advantages of DIDs is their ability to function independently of any organization or platform. In traditional identity systems, users are required to create accounts with service providers, linking their identity to a company's database. This reliance on external entities means that if a provider revokes an account, experiences a data breach, or ceases operations, users can lose access to their digital identity. DIDs eliminate this dependency by allowing individuals to generate their own unique identifiers that persist regardless of platform changes, corporate policies, or institutional control.

DIDs are closely linked to verifiable credentials, enabling individuals to present cryptographically signed proofs of identity without exposing unnecessary personal data. When a user receives a verifiable credential—such as a diploma, a professional certification, or a government-issued ID—they can associate it with their DID. When they need to verify their identity, they can present the credential along with their DID, allowing verifiers to confirm its authenticity without contacting the issuing authority. This decentralized verification process enhances privacy by reducing data exposure and minimizing the need for direct interactions with third parties.

One of the key technical innovations of DIDs is their compatibility with blockchain and distributed ledger technology (DLT). While DIDs do not store identity data directly on the blockchain, they use decentralized networks to register DID documents and enable secure identity resolution. By anchoring DIDs on blockchain networks, users can prove the integrity and existence of their identifier without relying on a centralized registry. This decentralized approach ensures that identity records cannot be altered or deleted without the owner's consent, providing a resilient and censorship-resistant identity framework.

DIDs are also designed for interoperability, allowing users to maintain a single decentralized identity across multiple platforms and services. Unlike proprietary identity solutions that lock users into specific ecosystems, DIDs follow open standards developed by organizations such as the World Wide Web Consortium (W3C). These standards ensure that DID-based identity systems can be used across different industries, from healthcare and finance to education and government services. By promoting a universal approach to decentralized identity, DIDs enable seamless authentication and verification across diverse digital environments.

Privacy is a critical aspect of decentralized identifiers, and DIDs offer several features to enhance user control over personal data. Unlike traditional identity models that require individuals to disclose extensive information to verify their identity, DIDs enable selective disclosure. Users can choose which identity attributes to share based on the context of a transaction, minimizing unnecessary data exposure. For example, a user proving they are over 18 for age-restricted services can do so without revealing their birthdate or other sensitive details. This privacy-preserving design is particularly important in an era where personal data is frequently collected, monetized, and exploited without user consent.

The implementation of DIDs is already gaining traction across various sectors. Governments are exploring decentralized identity solutions to provide digital citizen IDs that enhance security and reduce fraud. Financial institutions are integrating DIDs into know-your-customer (KYC) and anti-money laundering (AML) procedures to streamline compliance while protecting user privacy. Healthcare providers are leveraging DIDs to manage patient records securely, allowing individuals to control access to their medical history without relying on centralized databases. In the education sector, universities are issuing DID-based digital diplomas that students can share with employers without needing to request verification from the institution.

Despite their advantages, the widespread adoption of DIDs faces several challenges. One of the main obstacles is regulatory acceptance, as governments and institutions must recognize decentralized identifiers as valid forms of identity. Many existing legal frameworks are built around centralized identity issuance, making it difficult to integrate DIDs into regulatory compliance processes. While organizations such as the European Union and the United Nations are exploring decentralized identity standards, broader legal recognition is needed to ensure widespread adoption.

Another challenge is usability and accessibility. While DIDs offer significant security and privacy benefits, managing decentralized identifiers requires a level of technical literacy that may be unfamiliar to many users. Unlike traditional identity systems where passwords or recovery mechanisms are managed by service providers, DIDs rely on cryptographic keys that must be securely stored and managed by the user. If a user loses access to their private keys, recovering their DID can be complex, requiring multi-signature recovery or social recovery mechanisms. Efforts are being made to improve usability by developing intuitive identity wallets that simplify key management and authentication processes.

Scalability is another consideration in the adoption of DIDs. While blockchain networks provide a secure and decentralized foundation for DID management, high transaction costs and network congestion can create barriers to widespread implementation. Solutions such as layer 2 scaling, sidechains, and off-chain storage are being explored to improve efficiency and reduce costs associated with DID operations. Ensuring that decentralized identity systems can scale to support global adoption while maintaining security and decentralization remains a key focus for developers and organizations working on DID solutions.

The emergence of decentralized identifiers represents a transformative step toward self-sovereign identity, enabling individuals to control their digital presence without reliance on centralized authorities. By providing a decentralized, interoperable, and privacy-preserving identity framework, DIDs address many of the security and privacy challenges inherent in traditional identity systems. As technology evolves and regulatory frameworks adapt, DIDs have the potential to become a universal standard for digital identity, empowering individuals with greater control over their personal data while enhancing security and trust in the digital world.

Zero-Knowledge Proofs for Privacy-Preserving Identity

Zero-knowledge proofs (ZKPs) are a cryptographic method that enables one party to prove knowledge of a specific piece of information without revealing the actual data. In the context of identity management, ZKPs provide a way to authenticate and verify credentials without exposing personal details, making them a fundamental technology for privacy-preserving digital identity systems. As concerns over data privacy and security continue to grow, zero-knowledge proofs offer a powerful solution for minimizing data exposure while maintaining trust and verifiability in identity transactions.

Traditional identity verification processes require individuals to share significant amounts of personal information with third parties to prove eligibility for a service. For example, proving that one is of legal age typically involves presenting a driver's license or passport, revealing not only the date of birth but also the person's full name, address, and other unnecessary details. Similarly, proving employment status or financial eligibility often requires individuals to submit entire documents, exposing sensitive financial or professional data. This model poses serious privacy risks, as personal information is stored in centralized databases that are vulnerable to breaches, misuse, and unauthorized access.

Zero-knowledge proofs solve this problem by allowing individuals to verify specific identity attributes without disclosing the underlying information. Instead of revealing a full document, a person can generate a cryptographic proof that confirms they meet a specific requirement. For example, a zero-knowledge proof can demonstrate that an individual is over 18 years old without revealing their exact birth date or any other identifying details. This selective disclosure mechanism enhances privacy and security while maintaining the integrity of the verification process.

The fundamental concept behind zero-knowledge proofs is that a prover can convince a verifier that a statement is true without conveying any additional information. This is achieved through mathematical proofs that allow the verifier to confirm authenticity without learning the underlying data. The key properties of zero-knowledge proofs are completeness, soundness, and zero knowledge. Completeness ensures that if the statement is true, an honest verifier will be convinced. Soundness guarantees that a fraudulent prover cannot trick the verifier into accepting a false statement. Zero knowledge ensures that no extra information is revealed beyond the validity of the claim.

There are two main types of zero-knowledge proofs: interactive and non-interactive. Interactive zero-knowledge proofs require real-time interaction between the prover and the verifier, involving a back-and-forth exchange where the prover convinces the verifier step by step. While effective, this approach is less practical for large-scale identity systems due to its dependence on real-time communication. Non-interactive zero-knowledge proofs, on the other hand, allow the prover to generate a single proof that can be verified by anyone without requiring further interaction. These non-interactive proofs are more suitable for decentralized identity solutions, as they enable efficient and scalable verification.

One of the most widely used implementations of zero-knowledge proofs in identity management is zk-SNARKs (Zero-Knowledge Succinct Non-Interactive Arguments of Knowledge). zk-SNARKs enable compact, efficient, and non-interactive proofs that can be quickly verified without exposing sensitive data. This technology has been successfully applied in blockchain networks and decentralized identity frameworks to enhance privacy while maintaining verifiability. Another variation, zk-STARKs (Zero-Knowledge Scalable Transparent Arguments of Knowledge), improves upon zk-SNARKs by offering better scalability and transparency without requiring trusted setup procedures.

Decentralized identity systems leverage zero-knowledge proofs to enable privacy-preserving authentication. Instead of storing personal data in a centralized database, individuals hold their credentials in a digital wallet and generate zero-knowledge proofs when verification is required. For example, a user applying for a loan can prove they meet the income threshold without revealing their exact salary. Similarly, a job applicant can verify their university degree without disclosing the full transcript. This model shifts control from centralized authorities to individuals, reducing the risk of data breaches and identity theft.

Financial services can benefit greatly from zero-knowledge proofs by streamlining KYC (Know Your Customer) and AML (Anti-Money Laundering) processes while preserving user privacy. Banks and financial institutions are required to verify customer identities, often requiring them to collect and store sensitive personal information. This creates compliance burdens and security risks, as centralized databases become targets for cyberattacks. With zero-knowledge proofs, financial institutions can confirm regulatory compliance without storing excessive data. Customers can generate proofs that confirm their eligibility without disclosing their full identity, improving both privacy and security.

Zero-knowledge proofs also have applications in online authentication and access control. Traditional authentication methods rely on username-password combinations or multi-factor authentication, which often require users to submit personal credentials to service providers. This exposes users to phishing attacks, credential leaks, and unauthorized tracking. By integrating zero-knowledge proofs, authentication systems can verify identity attributes without transmitting raw credentials. A user could prove they have a valid subscription to a service without revealing their account details, reducing exposure to credential theft.

The healthcare industry presents another critical use case for zero-knowledge proofs in identity management. Patients often need to share medical records, insurance details, and vaccination certificates with healthcare providers, insurers, and regulatory agencies. These records contain highly sensitive information, and centralized storage increases the risk of data breaches. Zero-knowledge proofs allow patients to verify their medical history without exposing unnecessary details. For instance, a patient can prove they have received a required vaccination without sharing the complete medical record. This ensures compliance with healthcare regulations while maintaining strict privacy controls.

Governments and public sector organizations are also exploring zero-knowledge proofs for secure and privacy-preserving identity verification. Digital voting systems, for example, require a balance between voter anonymity and verifiability. Traditional electronic voting systems either expose voter identities or lack verifiability, creating trust issues. Zero-knowledge proofs enable a voting system where voters can prove their eligibility and cast their vote without revealing their identity or vote choice. This ensures fair and transparent elections while preserving voter privacy.

Despite their advantages, zero-knowledge proofs face challenges in implementation and adoption. The computational complexity of generating and verifying proofs can introduce performance bottlenecks, particularly in large-scale identity systems. Ongoing research and advancements in cryptographic techniques aim to optimize ZKP performance, making them more practical for real-world applications. Additionally, regulatory frameworks must adapt to accommodate privacy-preserving identity verification methods, ensuring legal recognition of zero-knowledge proofs in compliance processes.

Zero-knowledge proofs represent a transformative technology for privacy-preserving digital identity. By enabling secure verification without data exposure, they offer a solution to many of the privacy challenges associated with traditional identity management. As decentralized identity ecosystems continue to evolve, zero-knowledge proofs will play a crucial role in protecting user privacy, reducing reliance on centralized databases, and enabling secure, trustless authentication across various industries. The widespread adoption of zero-knowledge proofs has the potential to redefine digital interactions, shifting the balance of power from institutions to individuals while maintaining security and trust in an increasingly digital world.

The Role of Cryptography in Identity Security

Cryptography plays a foundational role in securing digital identities by enabling authentication, confidentiality, integrity, and non-repudiation. As digital interactions become more prevalent, protecting identity information from unauthorized access, fraud, and manipulation is critical. Traditional identity systems rely on centralized databases and passwords, which are vulnerable to data breaches, phishing attacks, and credential theft. Cryptographic techniques provide a more secure alternative by leveraging mathematical algorithms to protect identity data, ensure trusted verification, and enable secure communication. With the rise of decentralized identity systems, cryptography has become even more essential in ensuring privacy-preserving and tamper-resistant identity solutions.

One of the most widely used cryptographic techniques in identity security is public-key cryptography, also known as asymmetric encryption. In this system, each user has a pair of cryptographic keys: a public key and a private key. The public key is shared openly and can be used to encrypt messages or verify digital signatures, while the private key is kept secret and is used for decryption or signing data. This mechanism allows secure authentication without the need to transmit sensitive information. For example, when a user logs into a system using public-key cryptography, they can prove their identity by signing a challenge with their private key, which the system verifies using the corresponding public key. This process eliminates the need for passwords and reduces the risk of credential theft.

Digital signatures, which are based on public-key cryptography, are another crucial component of identity security. A digital signature is a cryptographic method used to verify the authenticity and integrity of digital documents, credentials, or transactions. When an entity issues a digital credential, it signs it using its private key, allowing verifiers to confirm its legitimacy using the corresponding public key. This ensures that the credential has not been altered and originates from a trusted source. Digital signatures are widely used in decentralized identity systems, electronic contracts, and blockchain-based identity verification, providing a secure way to establish trust without relying on central authorities.

Hash functions are another fundamental cryptographic tool in identity security. A hash function takes an input (such as a password, document, or identity record) and produces a fixed-length, unique hash value. Even a small change in the input results in a completely different hash, making it useful for verifying data integrity. In identity management, hash functions are often used to store passwords securely. Instead of storing plaintext passwords in a database, systems store hash values. When a user logs in, the entered password is hashed and compared to the stored hash, ensuring authentication without exposing sensitive data. Cryptographic hashing is also used in blockchain identity systems to create tamper-proof records, ensuring that identity data remains immutable and verifiable.

End-to-end encryption (E2EE) is a cryptographic technique that ensures that data remains confidential during transmission. In identity security, E2EE is used to protect sensitive communications and authentication processes from interception by third parties. Messaging applications, identity verification platforms, and secure login systems use E2EE to prevent attackers from eavesdropping on sensitive information. In decentralized identity systems, encryption is crucial for securing identity credentials stored in digital wallets, ensuring that only the rightful owner can access their data. By eliminating intermediaries and securing direct communication between users and verifiers, encryption strengthens privacy and reduces the risk of identity fraud.

Zero-knowledge proofs (ZKPs) are another cryptographic innovation that enhances identity security by allowing users to prove specific claims without revealing underlying information. Traditional identity verification processes require individuals to disclose personal details, increasing privacy risks. Zero-knowledge proofs enable selective disclosure, allowing users to verify their age, citizenship, or financial status without exposing sensitive data. For example, a user could prove they are over 18 without revealing their birth date. ZKPs are particularly valuable in decentralized identity systems, where privacy and security must be balanced with trust and authentication.

Decentralized identity frameworks leverage cryptographic techniques to eliminate reliance on centralized authorities while maintaining security and trust. In these systems, individuals control their identity credentials and present cryptographic proofs to verify their identity. Blockchain technology plays a crucial role in securing decentralized identity by using cryptographic hash functions and digital signatures to ensure the immutability and authenticity of identity records. Instead of storing identity data directly on the blockchain, decentralized identifiers (DIDs) and verifiable credentials are anchored using cryptographic techniques, allowing for secure and privacy-preserving identity verification.

Multi-factor authentication (MFA) is another security mechanism that relies on cryptographic principles to enhance identity protection. Traditional authentication methods that rely solely on passwords are highly vulnerable to attacks such as phishing and credential stuffing. MFA strengthens security by requiring multiple authentication factors, such as a password (something the user knows), a cryptographic key or smart card (something the user has), and biometric data (something the user is). Cryptographic techniques enable secure generation, storage, and verification of authentication tokens, ensuring that identity credentials cannot be easily compromised.

Biometric authentication systems also rely on cryptography to secure identity verification. Fingerprint scans, facial recognition, and iris scans are increasingly used for authentication, but biometric data must be protected against theft and misuse. Cryptographic methods such as homomorphic encryption and secure enclaves allow biometric data to be processed securely without exposing raw biometric information. These techniques ensure that even if biometric databases are breached, the stored templates remain protected and cannot be reconstructed into usable biometric data.

Despite its advantages, cryptography in identity security also presents challenges. The management of cryptographic keys is a significant concern, as losing a private key can result in the permanent loss of access to an identity or credential. Key recovery mechanisms, such as multi-signature schemes and social recovery methods, are being developed to mitigate this risk. Additionally, the computational complexity of cryptographic operations can impact system performance, requiring optimizations to ensure scalability and efficiency in large-scale identity systems.

The future of cryptographic identity security is closely tied to advancements in quantum computing. Traditional cryptographic algorithms, such as RSA and elliptic curve cryptography (ECC), rely on the difficulty of mathematical problems that quantum computers could eventually solve efficiently. Post-quantum cryptography (PQC) is an emerging field focused on developing cryptographic algorithms that remain secure against quantum attacks. As quantum computing continues to evolve, identity systems must adapt to ensure long-term security and resilience.

Cryptography is the backbone of modern identity security, enabling trusted authentication, privacy-preserving verification, and secure data storage. As digital identity continues to evolve, cryptographic techniques will play an increasingly critical role in ensuring security while empowering individuals with greater control over their personal information. Whether through encryption, digital signatures, zero-knowledge proofs, or decentralized identity frameworks, cryptography provides the tools necessary to build a more secure, private, and resilient identity ecosystem.

Identity Wallets: A User-Centric Approach

Identity wallets are a fundamental component of decentralized identity systems, enabling individuals to securely manage, store, and share their digital credentials without relying on centralized authorities. These wallets provide users with full control over their personal identity data, allowing them to authenticate themselves, prove credentials, and interact with services while maintaining privacy and security. Unlike traditional identity management systems, where third parties issue and control identity records, identity wallets operate under a self-sovereign model, putting the user at the center of their digital identity.

A digital identity wallet functions similarly to a physical wallet, but instead of holding cash, credit cards, and identification documents, it stores cryptographic credentials, decentralized identifiers (DIDs), and verifiable credentials (VCs). These digital assets allow users to prove their identity or specific attributes—such as age, nationality, or professional qualifications—without exposing unnecessary personal details. Identity wallets act as a secure interface between individuals and service providers, ensuring that identity verification is conducted with minimal data exposure.

One of the core benefits of identity wallets is the elimination of reliance on centralized identity providers. Traditional identity systems require individuals to create accounts with third-party services, linking their digital presence to organizations that control authentication processes. This creates significant risks, including data breaches, identity theft, and loss of control over personal information. With an identity wallet, users generate and manage their decentralized identifiers (DIDs) independently, allowing them to authenticate themselves without needing to rely on a single entity. This decentralization enhances security and reduces the risk of mass data leaks that are common in centralized identity databases.

Privacy is a key advantage of identity wallets, as they enable selective disclosure of personal information. Traditional identity verification methods often require users to provide more information than necessary. For example, proving eligibility for a service may require submitting a government-issued ID, which reveals a full name, date of birth, and address—even if only one of these attributes is required. Identity wallets leverage cryptographic techniques such as zero-knowledge proofs (ZKPs) to allow users to verify specific claims without exposing additional data. A user can prove they are over 18 without disclosing their birthdate, or verify their residency without revealing their exact address. This privacy-preserving approach minimizes the risk of data misuse and enhances user security.

Security is another critical feature of identity wallets, as they rely on cryptographic keys to ensure data integrity and authentication. Each identity wallet is protected by a private key, which is controlled exclusively by the user. This key is used to sign identity transactions and authenticate interactions with service providers. Unlike traditional password-based authentication systems, which are vulnerable to phishing attacks and credential theft, identity wallets eliminate the need for passwords by leveraging cryptographic authentication. However, key management remains a challenge, as losing a private key can result in the loss of access to one's digital identity. To address this issue, many identity wallets incorporate backup and recovery mechanisms, such as multi-signature authentication or social recovery, where trusted contacts can help restore access.

Interoperability is essential for identity wallets to function effectively across different platforms and services. The decentralized identity ecosystem consists of various stakeholders, including governments, businesses, financial institutions, and healthcare providers. To ensure seamless interactions, identity wallets must adhere to open standards, such as the World Wide Web Consortium's (W3C) Decentralized Identifiers (DIDs) and Verifiable Credentials (VCs) standards. These frameworks enable identity wallets to work across different industries and jurisdictions, allowing users to present their credentials in multiple contexts without being locked into a single ecosystem. Standardization efforts continue to play a crucial role in fostering widespread adoption and ensuring that identity wallets remain accessible and usable across various applications.

Identity wallets are already being integrated into various real-world use cases, demonstrating their potential to transform digital identity management. In the financial sector, banks and fintech companies are adopting identity wallets to streamline Know Your Customer (KYC) and Anti-Money Laundering (AML) compliance processes. Instead of requiring customers to submit identity documents repeatedly for verification, financial institutions can request a verifiable credential from an identity wallet. This approach enhances security, reduces onboarding friction, and protects user privacy.

In healthcare, identity wallets enable patients to manage their medical records and share them securely with healthcare providers, insurers, or research institutions. Patients can store verifiable health credentials, such as vaccination records, prescriptions, and test results, in their identity wallets and grant access only when necessary. This eliminates the need for centralized health data repositories, reducing the risk of data breaches while ensuring that sensitive medical information remains under the patient's control.

Government services are also benefiting from identity wallets, as they allow citizens to access digital public services securely. Digital IDs issued by governments can be stored in identity wallets, enabling individuals to prove their citizenship, residency, or voting eligibility without relying on paper-based documents. Countries exploring decentralized identity solutions, such as Estonia and Canada, are leveraging identity wallets to improve citizen authentication while maintaining privacy and security. These initiatives demonstrate the potential for identity wallets to enhance trust in digital governance and streamline interactions between individuals and public institutions.

In the employment sector, identity wallets are revolutionizing professional credentials and background verification. Job applicants can store verifiable credentials, such as academic degrees, certifications, and work experience, in their identity wallets. When applying for a job, they can share only the necessary credentials with employers, who can verify their authenticity instantly without contacting the issuing institutions. This eliminates resume fraud, accelerates hiring processes, and reduces administrative burdens for both job seekers and employers.

Despite their advantages, identity wallets face several challenges that must be addressed for widespread adoption. One of the primary concerns is user education and awareness. Many individuals are unfamiliar with decentralized identity concepts, and using an identity wallet requires understanding key management, cryptographic authentication, and selective disclosure. Efforts to improve user interfaces and provide intuitive onboarding experiences are essential to making identity wallets more accessible to non-technical users.

Regulatory compliance is another hurdle, as different jurisdictions have varying requirements for digital identity verification and data protection. While identity wallets offer enhanced privacy and security, governments and regulatory bodies must establish clear frameworks for recognizing decentralized identity credentials. Collaboration between technology providers, regulators, and policymakers is necessary to ensure that identity wallets comply with legal and compliance standards while maintaining the principles of self-sovereign identity.

Scalability is also a consideration, as identity wallets must handle a growing number of verifiable credentials across multiple industries and global networks. Ensuring that identity wallets remain efficient, responsive, and interoperable at scale requires continued advancements in cryptographic protocols, decentralized storage solutions, and blockchain-based identity frameworks.

Identity wallets represent a paradigm shift in digital identity management, placing users at the center of their identity interactions while enhancing security, privacy, and trust. As adoption continues to grow, identity wallets have the potential to become a universal tool for authentication, credential verification, and secure digital interactions, empowering individuals with greater control over their digital lives.

The Lifecycle of a Decentralized Identity

The lifecycle of a decentralized identity follows a structured process that ensures individuals maintain full control over their digital identities while interacting securely with various services. Unlike traditional identity systems that rely on centralized institutions to issue and verify credentials, decentralized identity systems empower users to create, manage, and authenticate their identities independently. This lifecycle consists of several key stages, including identity creation, issuance of verifiable credentials, authentication, usage, revocation, and recovery. Each stage is designed to enhance security, privacy, and user autonomy while minimizing reliance on intermediaries.

The first stage of the lifecycle is identity creation. In traditional identity systems, identities are assigned by governments, corporations, or institutions, but decentralized identity systems allow individuals to generate their own identities using decentralized identifiers (DIDs). A DID is a unique string of characters that acts as a persistent digital identifier, independent of any centralized authority. When a user creates a DID, a corresponding DID document is generated, containing cryptographic keys and metadata that define how the identity can be authenticated. This document is stored on a decentralized network, such as a blockchain or a distributed ledger, ensuring that the identity remains verifiable and tamper-proof without requiring a central repository.

Once an identity is created, the next stage involves obtaining verifiable credentials. Verifiable credentials (VCs) are digital attestations issued by trusted entities, such as governments, universities, banks, or employers. These credentials function similarly to physical documents like passports, diplomas, or professional certifications, but they are cryptographically signed to ensure authenticity and integrity. The issuer signs the credential using their private key, and the recipient stores it securely in their digital identity wallet. Since verifiable credentials are decentralized, they do not rely on a central database; instead, they can be verified against decentralized identity registries without direct involvement from the issuing authority.

Authentication and identity verification are the next steps in the lifecycle. When users need to prove their identity to access a service, they can present a verifiable credential through their digital wallet. The verifier, such as a bank, employer, or online platform, checks the credential's authenticity by validating its cryptographic signature and ensuring it has not been revoked. This process eliminates the need for traditional username-password combinations, reducing security risks such as phishing, credential theft, and unauthorized access. Additionally, cryptographic techniques like zero-knowledge proofs (ZKPs) allow users to verify specific attributes—such as their age, nationality, or employment status—without revealing unnecessary personal information, further enhancing privacy.

Identity usage occurs throughout a decentralized identity's lifespan. Unlike traditional identity systems where personal data is stored in multiple databases controlled by different service providers, decentralized identity allows individuals to interact with multiple entities using a single portable identity. For example, a user can use their decentralized identity to log into social media accounts, access financial services, enroll in online courses, or verify professional credentials, all without creating separate accounts for each service. This reduces the fragmentation of identity data, improves user experience, and enhances security by minimizing the attack surface for potential cyber threats.

Revocation is a critical aspect of the identity lifecycle, ensuring that credentials remain valid and trustworthy over time. In traditional identity systems, revocation processes are controlled by centralized authorities, often requiring manual intervention. In decentralized identity systems, revocation is handled through cryptographic mechanisms that allow issuers to update the status of a credential without modifying the entire credential itself. If a credential is revoked—such as when a professional license expires or a fraudulent claim is detected—the issuer records the revocation on a decentralized registry, allowing verifiers to check its validity in real time. This approach ensures that outdated or fraudulent credentials cannot be misused while maintaining the integrity of the overall identity system.

Identity recovery is one of the most challenging aspects of decentralized identity management. Unlike centralized systems where a forgotten password can be reset through email verification, decentralized identities rely on private cryptographic keys. If a user loses their private key, they risk losing access to their identity and credentials permanently. To address this issue, decentralized identity frameworks incorporate recovery mechanisms such as multi-signature authentication, where trusted contacts can help restore access, or social recovery models, where pre-approved guardians assist in key recovery. Secure backup solutions and hardware-based security modules also help users safeguard their identity credentials, reducing the risk of irreversible identity loss.

The final stage in the lifecycle of a decentralized identity is deactivation or identity retirement. Users may choose to deactivate their digital identity permanently, either due to account migration, compliance with data privacy regulations, or personal preference. In a decentralized model, identity deactivation does not involve deleting data from a central authority; instead, users can cryptographically prove that an identity is no longer in use while preserving historical verifiability. Organizations and services interacting with the identity can check for deactivation records, ensuring that only active identities remain valid within the ecosystem. This approach maintains security and trust while allowing users to control the longevity of their digital presence.

The lifecycle of a decentralized identity represents a fundamental shift from institutional control to user-centric management. Each stage— from identity creation to usage, revocation, and recovery—is designed to enhance security, privacy, and trust while reducing the need for centralized oversight. As decentralized identity solutions continue to evolve, advancements in cryptographic protocols, decentralized storage, and identity verification frameworks will further improve the usability and adoption of this model. By providing individuals with full control over their digital identity, decentralized identity systems empower users to navigate the digital world securely and independently, laying the foundation for a more private, user-controlled, and interoperable identity ecosystem.

Interoperability Challenges and Solutions

Interoperability is one of the most significant challenges in the implementation of decentralized identity systems. The ability for different identity solutions, platforms, and protocols to work seamlessly together is essential for the widespread adoption of self-sovereign identity (SSI) and decentralized identifiers (DIDs). Without interoperability, users and organizations may struggle to navigate multiple identity ecosystems, leading to fragmentation, inefficiency, and a lack of trust. Ensuring that decentralized identity frameworks can operate across different industries, jurisdictions, and technological infrastructures is critical to creating a global, user-centric identity system that is both functional and scalable.

One of the primary challenges in achieving interoperability is the existence of multiple identity standards. Various organizations and consortia have developed their own decentralized identity frameworks, each with its own protocols, data formats, and verification methods. While organizations such as the World Wide Web Consortium (W3C) have established common standards for decentralized identifiers (DIDs) and verifiable credentials (VCs), different implementations of these standards can still lead to compatibility issues. Identity providers, governments, and businesses adopting different blockchain networks or cryptographic methods may create identity silos that prevent seamless interactions across platforms.

Another major challenge is cross-platform integration. Many existing digital identity systems rely on centralized authentication mechanisms, such as OAuth, OpenID Connect, and SAML, which are widely used by enterprises, financial institutions, and government agencies. Integrating decentralized identity solutions with these legacy systems requires significant effort, as traditional identity providers are not designed to handle decentralized authentication models. Organizations that rely on centralized identity databases may resist transitioning to decentralized identity due to concerns about compatibility, regulatory compliance, and operational disruption.

Regulatory and jurisdictional differences also present a significant interoperability challenge. Governments and regulatory bodies have varying requirements for identity verification, data protection, and compliance. While decentralized identity frameworks emphasize user control and privacy, legal requirements such as Know Your Customer (KYC), Anti-Money Laundering (AML), and the General Data Protection Regulation (GDPR) impose constraints on how identity data can be managed and shared. Ensuring that decentralized identity solutions align with different regulatory frameworks while maintaining interoperability is a complex task that requires collaboration between policymakers, identity providers, and technology developers.

Another issue is the lack of universal trust anchors in decentralized identity ecosystems. In traditional identity systems, trust is established through centralized authorities such as governments, banks, and certification bodies. In decentralized identity, trust must be built through cryptographic proofs, decentralized identifiers, and verifiable credentials. However, different identity networks may implement their own trust frameworks, leading to inconsistencies in how identities and credentials are recognized across different ecosystems. Establishing a common framework for trust verification is crucial to ensuring that identities remain portable and usable across multiple platforms and jurisdictions.

Despite these challenges, several solutions are being developed to improve interoperability in decentralized identity systems. One of the most promising approaches is the adoption of open standards. The W3C Decentralized Identifiers (DID) and Verifiable Credentials (VC) specifications provide a foundation for interoperability by defining a common structure for identity data and verification methods. By adhering to these standards, identity providers and verifiers can ensure that credentials issued in one system can be recognized and validated in another.

Cross-chain identity solutions are also emerging as a way to bridge interoperability gaps between different blockchain networks. Since decentralized identity solutions often rely on blockchain or distributed ledger technology (DLT) for credential verification, the lack of interoperability between different blockchain ecosystems can create challenges. Cross-chain protocols and interoperability frameworks, such as decentralized identity hubs and blockchain bridges, enable identity credentials to be verified across multiple networks. These solutions help prevent identity lock-in to a single blockchain and allow users to maintain a portable identity across different platforms.

Federated trust frameworks are another approach to addressing interoperability challenges. These frameworks establish common guidelines for identity verification, credential issuance, and authentication across multiple identity ecosystems. Organizations such as the Sovrin Foundation, Hyperledger Indy, and Trust Over IP (ToIP) are working to create decentralized identity networks that interoperate while maintaining self-sovereign principles. By establishing shared governance models and trust registries, federated trust frameworks enable organizations and governments to recognize decentralized identities across different jurisdictions and industries.

Interoperability can also be improved through identity gateways that act as bridges between centralized and decentralized identity systems. These gateways allow organizations to integrate decentralized identity solutions into existing authentication and access management systems, enabling a gradual transition from traditional identity models to decentralized frameworks. For example, an enterprise that relies on Active Directory for authentication could implement an identity gateway that allows employees to use decentralized credentials without replacing the entire authentication infrastructure. This hybrid approach facilitates adoption by providing a smooth integration path for organizations transitioning to decentralized identity.

Another solution is the implementation of decentralized identity marketplaces, where issuers, holders, and verifiers can interact using standardized identity credentials. These marketplaces provide a way for identity stakeholders to exchange credentials, verify identities, and establish trust in a decentralized manner. By leveraging open protocols and standardized verification mechanisms, decentralized identity marketplaces enable cross-platform compatibility and reduce the friction associated with identity verification across different ecosystems.

Collaboration between industry stakeholders is essential to achieving full interoperability in decentralized identity systems. Governments, businesses, and technology providers must work together to establish common standards, align regulatory requirements, and develop scalable interoperability solutions. Initiatives such as the Decentralized Identity Foundation (DIF) and the European Blockchain Services Infrastructure (EBSI) are playing a crucial role in driving interoperability efforts by fostering collaboration between identity providers, standardization bodies, and regulatory agencies.

User experience is also a critical factor in ensuring the success of interoperable decentralized identity systems. While technical interoperability is essential, users must be able to manage and use their identities across different platforms effortlessly. Identity wallets that support multiple identity frameworks, intuitive user interfaces, and seamless authentication flows are necessary to encourage adoption. If users encounter friction when attempting to use decentralized identity solutions across various services, they may revert to traditional identity systems, limiting the potential of decentralized identity.

As decentralized identity adoption continues to grow, solving interoperability challenges will be key to ensuring a seamless, secure, and user-friendly identity ecosystem. Open standards, cross-chain identity solutions, federated trust frameworks, identity gateways, and industry collaboration all contribute to building an interoperable identity infrastructure. By prioritizing interoperability, decentralized identity systems can achieve widespread adoption, providing individuals with greater control over their digital identities while maintaining security, privacy, and trust across global digital interactions.

Identity Verification in a Decentralized World

Identity verification is a fundamental process that allows individuals to prove who they are to access services, conduct transactions, and establish trust in both digital and physical interactions. Traditional identity verification systems rely on centralized institutions such as governments, banks, and corporations to issue, validate, and store identity credentials. While these systems provide structured identity management, they also introduce risks such as data breaches, privacy violations, and exclusion of individuals who lack access to centralized identity systems. In a decentralized world, identity verification takes a different approach, leveraging cryptographic methods, blockchain technology, and self-sovereign identity (SSI) principles to enable a more secure, user-controlled, and privacy-preserving verification process.

Decentralized identity verification is based on the concept that individuals should have full control over their identity without needing to depend on third-party intermediaries. Unlike traditional models where users must repeatedly submit personal information to multiple service providers, decentralized identity systems allow users to store their identity credentials in digital wallets and present verifiable proofs when required. These credentials, issued by trusted entities such as governments, educational institutions, or employers, are cryptographically signed and stored securely, enabling users to verify their identity without exposing sensitive data.

A core component of decentralized identity verification is the use of decentralized identifiers (DIDs) and verifiable credentials (VCs). DIDs are unique, self-controlled digital identifiers that are not tied to a centralized authority. A user can create multiple DIDs for different purposes, maintaining privacy and reducing the risk of identity correlation across platforms. Verifiable credentials, on the other hand, serve as digital attestations that contain identity-related claims. For example, a university may issue a verifiable credential confirming that a person has earned a degree, or a government agency may issue a credential verifying citizenship. These credentials can be presented to verifiers, such as employers or financial institutions, who can confirm their authenticity without needing to contact the original issuer.

Blockchain technology plays a crucial role in decentralized identity verification by providing a tamper-proof, trustless verification mechanism. In a traditional identity system, verifiers must rely on centralized databases to check the validity of identity documents, requiring trust in the organization managing those databases. In a decentralized system, blockchain serves as a public ledger where cryptographic proofs of verifiable credentials can be recorded. This allows verifiers to confirm the integrity of credentials without directly accessing personal data, ensuring both security and privacy. Instead of storing sensitive identity information on the blockchain, only cryptographic hashes or decentralized registry entries are recorded, minimizing the risk of exposure while maintaining verifiability.

Privacy is a major concern in identity verification, and decentralized identity solutions offer several mechanisms to protect user data. One such technique is selective disclosure, which allows individuals to share only the minimum necessary information required for verification. In traditional identity verification, users often provide entire documents, such as passports or driver's licenses, even when only a small portion of the information is relevant. With selective disclosure, a user can prove they are above a certain age without revealing their exact birthdate or prove their employment status without disclosing their salary. This is achieved using cryptographic methods such as zero-knowledge proofs (ZKPs), which enable verification of specific claims without exposing the underlying data.

Decentralized identity verification has significant applications in various industries. In the financial sector, Know Your Customer (KYC) and Anti-Money Laundering (AML) compliance require banks and financial institutions to verify customer identities before allowing access to financial services. Traditional KYC processes involve repeated submission of identity documents, which can be cumbersome and pose security risks due to centralized data storage. With decentralized identity verification, individuals can present reusable verifiable credentials that prove compliance with KYC requirements without disclosing unnecessary personal information. This reduces compliance costs, minimizes fraud risks, and enhances user experience.

In healthcare, decentralized identity verification enables patients to manage and control their medical records while ensuring that healthcare providers can verify necessary credentials securely. For example, a patient can hold a verifiable credential for their vaccination status and share it with a hospital or pharmacy without revealing unrelated medical history. This improves patient privacy, prevents unauthorized access to sensitive health data, and ensures that verified medical information can be accessed efficiently when needed.

Governments and public services can also benefit from decentralized identity verification. Many government services, such as voting, social benefits distribution, and digital identity programs, require secure and reliable identity verification. A decentralized approach allows citizens to prove eligibility for services without relying on centralized identity databases that are prone to breaches and misuse. Digital voting systems, for example, can leverage decentralized identity verification to ensure that only eligible citizens can vote while maintaining voter anonymity. Similarly, social welfare programs can verify beneficiaries' eligibility without exposing unnecessary financial or personal information.

The workforce and education sectors are increasingly adopting decentralized identity verification for credential validation. Job applicants can present verifiable credentials issued by universities, certification bodies, or previous employers, allowing recruiters to instantly verify their qualifications without needing to contact issuing institutions. This eliminates credential fraud, speeds up hiring processes, and reduces administrative burdens for both employers and job seekers. Universities and training institutions can also issue digital diplomas and certificates as verifiable credentials, ensuring lifelong access to verified education records.

Despite its advantages, decentralized identity verification faces several challenges. One major hurdle is interoperability between different identity frameworks and standards. Various organizations and governments are developing decentralized identity solutions, but without common interoperability standards, users may face difficulties using their credentials across different platforms. Efforts by organizations such as the Decentralized Identity Foundation (DIF) and the World Wide Web Consortium (W3C) aim to create universal standards for DIDs and verifiable credentials to ensure seamless verification across different ecosystems.

Another challenge is user adoption and education. Many individuals are unfamiliar with decentralized identity concepts and may find managing cryptographic keys and digital wallets intimidating. To encourage adoption, decentralized identity solutions must prioritize user-friendly interfaces, clear instructions, and seamless integration with existing digital services. Educating users about the benefits of self-sovereign identity and providing intuitive recovery mechanisms for lost credentials will be crucial for widespread acceptance.

Regulatory compliance is another area of concern, as different jurisdictions have varying identity verification requirements. Governments and regulatory bodies must work together with technology providers to establish legal frameworks that recognize decentralized identity credentials as valid proofs of identity. Ensuring compliance with data protection laws, such as the General Data Protection Regulation (GDPR) and other regional privacy regulations, will be essential for integrating decentralized identity solutions into mainstream identity verification processes.

Decentralized identity verification represents a transformative shift in how individuals prove their identity while maintaining security, privacy, and control over their personal information. By eliminating the need for centralized authorities, leveraging cryptographic verification, and enabling selective disclosure, decentralized identity solutions offer a more efficient, user-centric approach to authentication. As technology advances and interoperability challenges are addressed, decentralized identity verification has the potential to redefine trust and security in digital interactions across industries and global systems.

Revocation and Recovery in Self-Sovereign Identity

Self-sovereign identity (SSI) provides individuals with full control over their digital identities, allowing them to manage credentials without reliance on centralized authorities. While this approach enhances privacy, security, and autonomy, it also introduces challenges related to credential revocation and identity recovery. Traditional identity systems handle these processes through centralized mechanisms, such as government agencies revoking passports or email providers resetting passwords. In decentralized identity ecosystems, revocation and recovery require alternative models that maintain user control while ensuring security, trust, and usability.

Revocation is the process of invalidating a previously issued verifiable credential. In traditional identity systems, institutions such as governments, universities, and banks manage revocation by maintaining centralized databases where credentials can be checked for validity. If an identity document is revoked—due to expiration, fraud, or policy violations—the institution updates its records and notifies relevant parties. However, in an SSI framework, credentials are held and managed by individuals rather than stored in central databases, making it necessary to design a decentralized method for tracking revocations while preserving privacy.

One approach to decentralized revocation is the use of cryptographic revocation registries. These registries do not store user identity data but instead maintain cryptographic proofs that indicate whether a credential is valid or revoked. When a credential issuer, such as a university or employer, decides to revoke a credential, they publish a cryptographic proof of revocation to a decentralized ledger, such as a blockchain. Verifiers checking the credential can reference this registry to determine if the credential is still valid without needing to contact the issuer directly. This ensures that revocation status can be verified in real time while protecting user privacy.

Another method for revocation is the use of status lists. In this model, issuers create a revocation list that assigns a cryptographic identifier to each issued credential. When a credential is revoked, its identifier is added to the status list, which is periodically updated and accessible to verifiers. This method ensures that verifiers can quickly determine credential validity while minimizing the risk of exposing personal data. To enhance privacy, status lists can be designed with zero-knowledge proofs (ZKPs), allowing users to prove that their credential is not revoked without revealing which credential they hold.

Revocation presents additional challenges when dealing with credentials that require ongoing verification, such as professional licenses, academic degrees, or security clearances. In these cases, institutions may issue time-limited credentials that must be reverified periodically. Instead of maintaining an active revocation list, the system can use short-lived credentials that expire automatically after a set period, requiring reissuance for continued validity. This method reduces reliance on revocation registries while ensuring that credentials remain current and trusted.

Recovery is another critical aspect of SSI, addressing situations where users lose access to their digital identities. In traditional identity systems, account recovery is managed by centralized entities through password resets, email verification, or customer support assistance. In SSI, individuals control their cryptographic keys, which are essential for accessing and managing identity credentials. If a user loses their private key, they risk losing access to their entire digital identity, including verifiable credentials stored in their identity wallet. Designing effective recovery mechanisms is therefore essential to ensuring the usability and reliability of decentralized identity systems.

One common approach to decentralized identity recovery is the use of multi-signature (multi-sig) authentication. In this model, users can designate multiple trusted parties—such as family members, colleagues, or institutions—as key recovery agents. If the user loses access to their private key, these trusted parties can collectively help regenerate access by providing their cryptographic signatures. This process, known as social recovery, ensures that identity recovery does not depend on a single entity while maintaining a decentralized and trust-based approach.

Secret sharing is another method used for identity recovery. This technique, based on Shamir's Secret Sharing algorithm, splits a private key into multiple fragments, distributing them among trusted individuals or secure storage locations. To recover the key, a predefined number of fragments must be combined, ensuring that no single party has full control over the identity. This method provides resilience against key loss while preventing unauthorized access by any single entity.

Some identity wallets implement biometric-based recovery solutions, where a user's biometrics, such as fingerprints or facial recognition, are used to unlock access to their identity credentials. While biometric authentication enhances usability, it also introduces privacy concerns, as biometric data must be securely stored and protected against misuse. To mitigate these risks, biometric-based recovery can be combined with multi-factor authentication (MFA) or secure enclaves that encrypt biometric data without exposing it to external threats.

Another emerging approach to identity recovery involves decentralized backup mechanisms. Users can store encrypted backups of their private keys on distributed networks, such as decentralized cloud storage or blockchain-based identity vaults. These backups can be accessed only with the user's authorization, ensuring that recovery is possible even if the original device or wallet is lost. Secure backup solutions prevent identity loss while maintaining privacy and security in a decentralized environment.

Despite the availability of recovery mechanisms, user education and awareness play a crucial role in ensuring effective identity management. Unlike centralized identity systems, where password resets and customer support provide a safety net, SSI requires users to take greater responsibility for their credentials and recovery keys. Providing clear guidance on key management, recovery options, and best practices is essential for preventing identity loss and ensuring a seamless user experience.

The balance between security and usability remains a key challenge in designing decentralized revocation and recovery mechanisms. Overly complex recovery solutions may discourage adoption, while inadequate security measures can lead to identity theft or unauthorized access. Identity systems must strike a balance by providing robust security while maintaining user-friendly recovery options that accommodate a wide range of technical literacy levels.

As decentralized identity adoption continues to grow, the development of standardized revocation and recovery frameworks will be essential for ensuring trust and reliability. Collaboration between identity providers, developers, and regulatory bodies will play a crucial role in establishing best practices and technical standards for managing revocation and recovery in SSI ecosystems. Ensuring that identity credentials remain verifiable, recoverable, and secure will ultimately enhance the adoption and long-term success of self-sovereign identity systems.

Decentralized Identity Governance Models

Governance is a crucial component of any identity system, ensuring trust, security, and compliance within a given framework. Traditional identity governance models rely on centralized authorities such as governments, financial institutions, and corporations to issue, verify, and revoke identity credentials. While these models provide structure and oversight, they also create challenges related to user privacy, security risks, and dependency on intermediaries. Decentralized identity governance seeks to establish trust without requiring central control, leveraging cryptographic verification, distributed ledger technology, and community-driven decision-making processes to ensure secure and user-controlled identity management.

A decentralized identity governance model is designed to provide a framework for how decentralized identifiers (DIDs) and verifiable credentials (VCs) are issued, verified, and managed in a trustless environment. Unlike centralized governance models, which depend on an authoritative entity, decentralized governance distributes decision-making across multiple stakeholders, ensuring that identity systems remain resilient, inclusive, and adaptable. These models define the policies, protocols, and standards that ensure interoperability, security, and compliance across decentralized identity ecosystems.

One of the foundational components of decentralized identity governance is trust frameworks. A trust framework establishes the rules, policies, and agreements that guide how identity credentials are issued, exchanged, and verified. These frameworks define the roles of issuers, holders, and verifiers, ensuring that credentials remain secure and verifiable across different platforms and jurisdictions. Trust frameworks may be developed by industry groups, governmental organizations, or decentralized autonomous organizations (DAOs) to provide consistent and transparent identity governance.

Decentralized identity governance often operates under the principle of self-sovereign identity (SSI), which emphasizes user control over identity credentials without reliance on intermediaries. This governance model ensures that individuals can create, manage, and share their identities independently while adhering to decentralized trust mechanisms. To facilitate trust, decentralized identity networks rely on public-key cryptography, blockchain registries, and cryptographic proofs to authenticate identity claims without exposing unnecessary personal information.

Decentralized autonomous organizations (DAOs) play a growing role in decentralized identity governance, providing a community-driven approach to decision-making. DAOs enable stakeholders to participate in governance processes through voting mechanisms, ensuring that identity policies and standards evolve in a democratic and transparent manner. By leveraging smart contracts and blockchain technology, DAOs automate governance rules, reducing reliance on centralized entities while maintaining accountability within the identity ecosystem. This approach ensures that governance decisions are collectively managed by network participants rather than dictated by a single organization.

Interoperability is a key challenge in decentralized identity governance, as different identity networks, blockchain protocols, and verification mechanisms must work seamlessly together. Governance models must establish common technical and policy standards to ensure that decentralized identity solutions can be used across multiple industries and jurisdictions. Organizations such as the World Wide Web Consortium (W3C), the Decentralized Identity Foundation (DIF), and the Trust Over IP Foundation (ToIP) are actively developing governance frameworks to promote standardization and compatibility among decentralized identity systems.

Compliance with legal and regulatory requirements is another critical aspect of decentralized identity governance. Governments and regulatory bodies impose various identity verification and data protection regulations, such as Know Your Customer (KYC), Anti-Money Laundering (AML), and the General Data Protection Regulation (GDPR). Decentralized governance models must align with these regulations while preserving user privacy and security. Privacy-enhancing technologies such as zero-knowledge proofs (ZKPs) and selective disclosure enable compliance without requiring full identity exposure, ensuring that decentralized identity systems meet legal requirements while maintaining decentralization principles.

Decentralized governance models also address credential issuance and revocation processes. In traditional systems, centralized authorities maintain control over credential issuance, allowing them to revoke credentials if necessary. In a decentralized framework, governance models must define how credentials can be revoked in a way that maintains trust while preventing misuse. Cryptographic revocation registries and status lists allow verifiers to check the validity of credentials without requiring direct communication with issuers.

These mechanisms ensure that credentials remain trustworthy while respecting user privacy and autonomy.

Identity verification in decentralized governance models relies on verifiable credential issuers and decentralized reputation systems. Instead of depending on a single authority, decentralized identity networks enable multiple trusted issuers to provide credentials based on predefined governance rules. Verifiers can then assess credential validity based on cryptographic proofs rather than institutional trust. Additionally, decentralized reputation systems enable users to build trust over time through verified interactions, allowing them to establish credibility within a decentralized identity ecosystem.

Decentralized identity governance must also account for the role of identity wallets, which serve as the primary interface for users to manage their credentials. Governance frameworks define how identity wallets interact with verifiable credentials, ensuring security, usability, and interoperability. Secure key management, credential portability, and user consent mechanisms are essential components of identity wallet governance, ensuring that individuals retain full control over their digital identities while maintaining compliance with trust frameworks.

Scalability is another consideration in decentralized identity governance. Traditional identity systems operate under controlled environments, allowing for structured scaling. Decentralized identity, however, must handle millions of users, credentials, and verification requests without relying on central infrastructure. Governance models must establish efficient protocols for managing large-scale identity interactions while maintaining decentralized security and performance. Layer 2 scaling solutions, distributed identity registries, and decentralized storage mechanisms contribute to the scalability of decentralized identity networks.

The evolution of decentralized identity governance requires collaboration between governments, private organizations, and decentralized technology providers. While decentralized identity aims to reduce reliance on centralized institutions, governance frameworks must still interact with existing regulatory and institutional infrastructures. Public-private partnerships and regulatory sandboxes provide an opportunity for decentralized identity projects to test governance models in real-world environments, ensuring that decentralized identity solutions can coexist with traditional identity systems.

Decentralized identity governance represents a shift toward user-centric identity management, balancing security, privacy, and compliance within a distributed trust framework. As decentralized identity adoption grows, governance models will continue to evolve, incorporating new technologies, regulatory requirements, and industry standards. Ensuring that decentralized identity governance remains transparent, inclusive, and adaptable will be key to building a secure and trustworthy digital identity ecosystem that empowers individuals while maintaining institutional trust.

Identity Trust Anchors and Their Importance

Trust is a fundamental requirement in identity systems, ensuring that individuals, organizations, and service providers can rely on the authenticity and integrity of identity claims. In both centralized and decentralized identity models, trust anchors play a critical role in verifying and maintaining confidence in identity credentials. A trust anchor is an entity or mechanism that serves as a foundational source of trust, validating identity-related information in a way that others can recognize and accept. These anchors can be government agencies, financial institutions, certification authorities, or decentralized mechanisms that enable trust without requiring centralized control.

In traditional identity systems, trust anchors are often centralized institutions that issue identity credentials such as passports, driver's licenses, and birth certificates. These documents serve as widely accepted proof of identity because they are issued by trusted entities that follow standardized verification processes. When a person presents a government-issued ID to open a bank account or board a flight, the trust anchor behind that document (the government) provides assurance that the identity claim is valid. Centralized trust anchors create a structured and recognized system of identity verification, but they also introduce risks such as single points of failure, privacy concerns, and exclusion for individuals without access to government-issued credentials.

Decentralized identity models aim to replace or complement traditional trust anchors with distributed trust mechanisms. Instead of relying on a single authoritative source, decentralized identity systems leverage cryptographic proofs, verifiable credentials, and decentralized identifiers (DIDs) to establish trust. In these models, trust anchors can take various forms, including blockchain-based registries, reputation-based networks, and decentralized certification authorities. By removing the need for central control, decentralized trust anchors enhance security, reduce fraud, and give individuals more control over their identities.

One of the key advantages of decentralized trust anchors is their ability to prevent identity fraud and forgery. Traditional identity documents can be physically stolen, forged, or manipulated, making identity theft a widespread problem. In contrast, decentralized identity systems use cryptographic signatures and immutable records to ensure that credentials cannot be altered or duplicated. When a verifiable credential is issued by a trust anchor, it is signed using the issuer's private key, allowing verifiers to confirm its authenticity using the corresponding public key. This process ensures that identity credentials remain tamper-proof and verifiable without needing direct communication with the issuing entity.

Trust anchors in decentralized identity systems are not limited to government entities. Private organizations, educational institutions, and industry groups can also serve as trust anchors by issuing credentials that are recognized within specific ecosystems. For example, universities can issue verifiable credentials for academic degrees, professional organizations can issue certifications for licensed professionals, and financial institutions can issue digital KYC (Know Your Customer) credentials for banking and financial services. By expanding the range of trust anchors beyond government agencies, decentralized identity systems create a more inclusive and diverse identity verification ecosystem.

Reputation-based trust anchors are another emerging model in decentralized identity. Instead of relying solely on institutional credentials, individuals can build trust over time through verified interactions, endorsements, and transaction histories. This approach is particularly useful for individuals who lack formal identity documents but can demonstrate credibility through community validation. For example, in peer-to-peer marketplaces, ride-sharing platforms, and freelance networks, users develop reputation scores based on verified interactions. Decentralized identity systems can incorporate reputation-based trust anchors, allowing individuals to establish trustworthiness through cryptographically signed attestations from peers and previous transactions.

Blockchain technology provides an additional layer of security and transparency for trust anchors. In decentralized identity systems, trust anchors can use blockchain networks to register identity attestations, ensuring that they remain immutable and accessible for verification. By anchoring identity credentials on a blockchain, trust anchors create a tamper-proof record that can be referenced by verifiers without exposing personal data. This approach enhances the reliability of identity verification while preserving user privacy, as only cryptographic proofs are stored on the blockchain rather than sensitive identity details.

Interoperability is a critical consideration for trust anchors in decentralized identity systems. Identity credentials issued by one trust anchor should be recognized and accepted across multiple platforms, industries, and jurisdictions. For this to be possible, decentralized identity frameworks must adhere to open standards such as the World Wide Web Consortium (W3C) Verifiable Credentials standard and the Decentralized Identifiers (DID) specification. By ensuring interoperability, decentralized trust anchors enable seamless identity verification across global digital ecosystems, reducing friction and enhancing user convenience.

Regulatory compliance is another important aspect of identity trust anchors. Governments and regulatory bodies impose strict identity verification requirements, particularly in industries such as finance, healthcare, and law enforcement. Decentralized trust anchors must align with these regulations while preserving privacy and decentralization principles. Privacy-enhancing technologies such as zero-knowledge proofs (ZKPs) enable decentralized identity systems to meet regulatory requirements without compromising user autonomy. For example, an individual can prove they meet age or income eligibility criteria without revealing their full identity details, ensuring compliance with regulations while minimizing data exposure.

Challenges remain in the adoption of decentralized trust anchors. One key issue is the need for widespread recognition and acceptance of decentralized credentials. Traditional institutions may be hesitant to adopt decentralized identity models due to concerns about security, fraud prevention, and legal recognition. To address this, decentralized identity ecosystems must build strong networks of trust anchors that are widely accepted across different sectors. Public-private partnerships, industry collaborations, and regulatory engagement are essential for increasing adoption and ensuring that decentralized trust anchors are seen as legitimate and reliable sources of identity verification.

Another challenge is user awareness and trust. Many individuals are accustomed to traditional identity verification methods and may be unfamiliar with decentralized identity concepts. Educating users about how decentralized trust anchors work, how to verify credentials securely, and how to manage their own digital identities is crucial for adoption. User-friendly identity wallets and authentication interfaces must be developed to make decentralized identity systems accessible to a broad audience.

Identity trust anchors are a foundational element of decentralized identity systems, enabling secure, verifiable, and privacy-preserving identity verification. By shifting trust from centralized authorities to cryptographic proofs, distributed registries, and reputation-based networks, decentralized identity models enhance security, reduce fraud, and give individuals greater control over their identities. As decentralized trust anchors continue to evolve, their adoption and integration into global digital ecosystems will play a crucial role in shaping the future of identity verification and trust.

The Role of Governments in Self-Sovereign Identity

Governments have traditionally played a central role in identity management, acting as the primary issuers of identity documents such as passports, birth certificates, driver's licenses, and national ID cards. These documents are widely accepted as proof of identity and serve as the foundation for accessing essential services, from banking and healthcare to voting and social security. As digital interactions continue to expand, traditional identity models face increasing challenges related to security, privacy, and accessibility. Self-sovereign identity (SSI) presents an alternative approach that shifts control from centralized authorities to individuals, allowing them to manage their own digital identities. While SSI is designed to reduce dependence on intermediaries, governments still play a crucial role in the adoption, regulation, and integration of decentralized identity systems.

One of the key responsibilities of governments in the context of SSI is establishing legal recognition for decentralized identities. Traditional identity systems are backed by legal frameworks that define how identity credentials are issued, verified, and used in official transactions. For self-sovereign identity to gain mainstream acceptance, governments must define regulatory standards that recognize digital credentials issued through decentralized identity frameworks. Without legal recognition, individuals may struggle to use self-sovereign identities for critical services such as voting, taxation, and law enforcement interactions. Some governments are already exploring decentralized identity solutions, working to create regulatory frameworks that balance security, privacy, and compliance with existing laws.

Governments also play a crucial role in ensuring interoperability between self-sovereign identity systems and existing public sector services. Many citizens rely on government-issued identities to access healthcare, education, and social benefits. If decentralized identity solutions are to be adopted at scale, they must integrate seamlessly with government databases and service providers. Governments can facilitate this integration by adopting open standards such as the World Wide Web Consortium's (W3C) Decentralized Identifiers

(DIDs) and Verifiable Credentials (VCs) specifications. By ensuring that decentralized identity systems are compatible with existing infrastructure, governments can prevent fragmentation and promote widespread adoption.

Another significant area of involvement for governments is identity verification and trust anchoring. While SSI allows individuals to create and manage their own digital identities, the legitimacy of these identities often depends on trusted issuers. Governments, as the primary issuers of official identity documents, can serve as trust anchors by issuing verifiable credentials in a decentralized manner. For example, a government could issue a digital passport or a national ID as a verifiable credential that individuals store in their identity wallets. This would allow users to authenticate their identity in a privacy-preserving way without relying on centralized databases. By leveraging blockchain technology and cryptographic methods, governments can ensure that verifiable credentials remain secure, tamper-proof, and easily verifiable without exposing unnecessary personal data.

Privacy protection is another critical responsibility of governments in the SSI ecosystem. Traditional identity models often require individuals to share excessive personal information with service providers, leading to data breaches, identity theft, and unauthorized surveillance. Self-sovereign identity addresses these concerns by allowing users to disclose only the minimum necessary information using cryptographic proofs, such as zero-knowledge proofs (ZKPs). Governments must establish policies that reinforce privacy-preserving identity solutions and prohibit the misuse of personal data. Ensuring compliance with privacy regulations such as the General Data Protection Regulation (GDPR) and similar frameworks can help build public trust in decentralized identity systems.

Governments can also use self-sovereign identity solutions to improve the efficiency and security of public services. Many government processes still rely on paper-based identity verification, which is slow, costly, and prone to fraud. By adopting decentralized identity systems, governments can streamline service delivery, reduce administrative overhead, and enhance security. For example, digital voting systems that leverage SSI can ensure voter authentication while preserving anonymity, reducing the risk of election fraud. Similarly, decentralized identity verification can simplify tax filing, social benefit distribution, and healthcare record management, improving accessibility and reducing bureaucratic inefficiencies.

One of the major challenges governments face in adopting SSI is the need to balance decentralization with regulatory oversight. While self-sovereign identity promotes user control and minimizes reliance on centralized authorities, governments must still ensure that identity systems comply with national security, anti-fraud, and anti-money laundering (AML) regulations. Law enforcement agencies require mechanisms to prevent identity fraud, track financial crimes, and enforce legal compliance. Governments must find ways to integrate SSI solutions while maintaining the ability to investigate and respond to fraudulent activities. This may involve developing decentralized identity registries that enable lawful verification without violating user privacy.

Digital inclusion is another area where governments can contribute to the success of self-sovereign identity. Millions of people around the world lack official identity documents, preventing them from accessing essential services such as banking, healthcare, and education. Traditional identity systems often exclude marginalized populations, such as refugees, undocumented workers, and individuals in remote areas. Self-sovereign identity offers a solution by allowing individuals to establish a digital identity independently. However, governments must actively support initiatives that promote digital identity inclusion, ensuring that decentralized identity solutions are accessible to all citizens, regardless of socioeconomic status or technological literacy.

Governments also have a role to play in fostering public-private collaboration in the development of SSI ecosystems. Decentralized identity solutions require cooperation between governments, businesses, technology providers, and civil society organizations. Public-private partnerships can help create trusted digital identity networks that align with regulatory requirements while maintaining user control and privacy. Governments can support SSI innovation by funding research, facilitating pilot programs, and providing regulatory sandboxes where decentralized identity solutions can be tested in real-world environments.

Education and awareness are also critical to the successful adoption of self-sovereign identity. Many citizens and businesses are unfamiliar with decentralized identity concepts, making it essential for governments to provide clear guidance on how SSI works, its benefits, and best practices for secure identity management. Governments can develop public education campaigns, offer digital identity training programs, and integrate SSI awareness into broader cybersecurity initiatives. Ensuring that citizens understand and trust decentralized identity solutions is key to driving adoption and preventing misuse.

As decentralized identity technology continues to evolve, governments must navigate the complexities of integrating SSI into existing regulatory, legal, and technological frameworks. While SSI reduces reliance on centralized authorities, governments remain essential in establishing trust, ensuring interoperability, protecting privacy, and promoting digital inclusion. By embracing decentralized identity principles and supporting open, user-centric identity ecosystems, governments can play a pivotal role in shaping the future of digital identity in a way that benefits individuals, businesses, and society as a whole.

Identity Proofing and Attestation Mechanisms

Identity proofing and attestation mechanisms are fundamental components of digital identity systems, ensuring that individuals and entities can verify their credentials securely and reliably. Traditional identity proofing relies on centralized authorities such as governments, financial institutions, and businesses to validate an individual's identity before granting access to services. However, as digital interactions become more decentralized, new approaches to identity proofing and attestation are emerging, leveraging cryptographic verification, verifiable credentials, and decentralized identifiers (DIDs) to enhance security, privacy, and trust.

Identity proofing is the process of establishing that an individual or entity is who they claim to be. This process typically involves collecting identity documents, biometric data, or other proof-of-identity factors, which are then validated against authoritative sources. In traditional identity systems, this process is often manual and requires a trusted intermediary to verify credentials. For example, opening a bank account usually requires a passport or government-issued ID, along with secondary proofs such as a utility bill or employment verification. While effective, this centralized approach presents challenges such as data breaches, identity fraud, and lack of user control over personal information.

In a decentralized identity model, identity proofing shifts from reliance on central authorities to a distributed trust framework where credentials are issued and verified through cryptographic means. Decentralized identity systems use verifiable credentials (VCs) to allow users to prove their identity without exposing excessive personal data. Instead of presenting a physical document or a scanned ID, individuals receive a digital credential signed by a trusted issuer, which can be stored in a digital wallet and presented when required. This approach enhances security by reducing the need for centralized data storage while enabling faster and more privacy-preserving identity verification.

Attestation mechanisms play a critical role in decentralized identity systems by providing a way to validate claims made by an individual or organization. An attestation is a statement made by a trusted entity— such as a government, employer, or university—confirming the authenticity of an identity attribute. For example, a university may issue an attestation confirming that a student has graduated with a specific degree, or a government may issue an attestation verifying an individual's age for legal purposes. These attestations are cryptographically signed, allowing verifiers to check their authenticity without needing to contact the original issuer.

One of the key benefits of attestation mechanisms in decentralized identity systems is selective disclosure. Traditional identity proofing often requires individuals to share unnecessary information. For example, proving eligibility for an age-restricted service typically requires showing a government-issued ID, which exposes full name, date of birth, and other details. With selective disclosure, users can prove that they meet a requirement—such as being over 18—without revealing any additional personal information. This is made possible through cryptographic techniques such as zero-knowledge proofs

(ZKPs), which allow an individual to prove a statement is true without revealing the underlying data.

Biometric verification is another method used in identity proofing, providing a strong link between an individual and their digital identity. Biometric factors such as fingerprints, facial recognition, and iris scans can be used to verify that a person is who they claim to be. In decentralized identity systems, biometric data is not stored in a central database but rather kept under the user's control, typically within a secure enclave on their personal device. This ensures that biometric verification remains privacy-preserving while providing a reliable method of identity proofing without relying on passwords or traditional authentication methods.

Decentralized identity proofing also benefits from blockchain technology, which ensures the integrity and security of identity attestations. While personal identity data is not stored directly on the blockchain, cryptographic hashes of verifiable credentials can be recorded, enabling instant and tamper-proof verification. This means that an employer or financial institution can verify an individual's credentials without relying on a central registry or directly contacting the issuer. The decentralized nature of blockchain ensures that identity proofs cannot be altered or revoked without proper authorization, reducing fraud risks and increasing trust in digital interactions.

One of the biggest challenges in decentralized identity proofing is establishing universally recognized trust anchors. Traditional identity systems depend on widely accepted institutions such as governments and banks to issue identity credentials. In a decentralized model, the legitimacy of identity proofing depends on a network of trust anchors that validate credentials based on open standards and cryptographic verification rather than institutional authority. This requires collaboration between governments, businesses, and technology providers to create interoperable identity frameworks that work across different jurisdictions and industries.

Another challenge is ensuring inclusivity in identity proofing processes. Millions of people worldwide lack formal identity documents, making it difficult for them to participate in digital and financial systems. Decentralized identity proofing offers a solution by allowing individuals to build their identity through alternative means, such as community attestations, social trust networks, or transaction histories. In this model, individuals who lack government-issued IDs can receive verifiable credentials from trusted community members or organizations, gradually establishing a reputation that can be used for broader identity verification.

The role of artificial intelligence (AI) in identity proofing is also expanding. AI-powered identity verification tools can analyze facial biometrics, document authenticity, and behavioral patterns to detect fraudulent activities. In decentralized identity systems, AI can be used to enhance fraud detection while maintaining privacy by processing data locally on user devices rather than central servers. AI-driven identity proofing can improve accessibility and accuracy, particularly in large-scale identity verification scenarios such as remote onboarding for financial services or cross-border identity validation.

Regulatory compliance remains a key factor in identity proofing and attestation mechanisms. While decentralized identity systems offer privacy advantages, they must also comply with legal frameworks such as Know Your Customer (KYC), Anti-Money Laundering (AML), and the General Data Protection Regulation (GDPR). Decentralized identity solutions must balance the need for compliance with the principles of user sovereignty and privacy. Innovations such as privacy-preserving attestations, decentralized KYC frameworks, and regulatory sandboxes are being explored to ensure that decentralized identity proofing meets legal requirements while maintaining user control.

The shift from centralized to decentralized identity proofing represents a fundamental change in how identity is verified in the digital world. By leveraging verifiable credentials, cryptographic attestations, blockchain technology, and privacy-enhancing techniques, decentralized identity systems provide a more secure, user-centric approach to identity verification. As adoption increases, ongoing collaboration between governments, industry leaders, and technology innovators will be essential to ensuring that identity proofing mechanisms remain interoperable, trustworthy, and accessible to all.

Risks and Threats to Decentralized Identity

Decentralized identity represents a paradigm shift in how individuals manage and control their digital identities, moving away from centralized authorities and toward user sovereignty. While this model offers significant benefits in terms of privacy, security, and interoperability, it also introduces several risks and threats that must be addressed to ensure its long-term viability. These challenges range from security vulnerabilities and regulatory concerns to usability issues and potential misuse of decentralized identity systems.

One of the most significant risks associated with decentralized identity is private key management. In traditional identity systems, institutions manage and store user credentials, allowing for account recovery mechanisms such as password resets. In a decentralized identity system, users control their own cryptographic private keys, which serve as the foundation of their digital identity. Losing a private key can result in permanent identity loss, making it impossible for users to recover their credentials or verify their identity. Malicious actors may also attempt to steal private keys through phishing attacks, malware, or social engineering tactics, potentially compromising an individual's entire digital identity.

Another major threat is identity fraud and impersonation. While decentralized identity systems rely on cryptographic verification to establish trust, attackers may attempt to create fraudulent identities using falsified credentials. Without robust identity proofing mechanisms, decentralized identity networks could become vulnerable to synthetic identity fraud, where attackers generate entirely new digital personas that do not correspond to real individuals. Decentralized identity solutions must implement strong verification processes, such as biometric authentication, verifiable credentials, and zero-knowledge proofs, to prevent fraud and ensure that only legitimate identities are recognized.

Scalability and performance issues also present challenges for decentralized identity systems. Many decentralized identity solutions rely on blockchain technology or distributed ledger systems to store and verify credentials. While these technologies provide security and immutability, they can also introduce latency, high transaction costs, and limited scalability. Blockchain networks may experience congestion during peak usage periods, making identity verification slower and less efficient. Additionally, decentralized identity systems must ensure that verification processes remain cost-effective, as high transaction fees could discourage widespread adoption.

Regulatory and compliance risks are another area of concern. Decentralized identity systems operate across multiple jurisdictions, each with its own legal and regulatory requirements. Privacy laws such as the General Data Protection Regulation (GDPR) in Europe impose strict guidelines on how personal data is collected, stored, and processed. While decentralized identity aims to enhance privacy by minimizing data exposure, it must also comply with legal frameworks that govern identity verification, anti-money laundering (AML) measures, and know-your-customer (KYC) regulations. Governments and regulatory bodies may struggle to adapt existing legal structures to accommodate decentralized identity models, leading to potential conflicts between privacy principles and legal obligations.

Another risk is the potential misuse of decentralized identity systems by malicious actors. While self-sovereign identity (SSI) promotes user control and privacy, it can also provide anonymity to individuals engaging in illegal activities. Criminal organizations could use decentralized identity to create untraceable identities for illicit transactions, money laundering, or fraud. Ensuring that decentralized identity systems include mechanisms for lawful oversight, while still preserving user privacy, is a delicate balance that developers and policymakers must address.

Interoperability challenges also pose a risk to decentralized identity adoption. Various organizations and technology providers are developing their own decentralized identity solutions, each with different technical standards, blockchain platforms, and governance models. Without standardized interoperability frameworks, users may find it difficult to use their decentralized credentials across different services, limiting the practical benefits of self-sovereign identity. Efforts by organizations such as the Decentralized Identity Foundation (DIF) and the World Wide Web Consortium (W3C) are working to establish common identity standards, but widespread adoption of these standards remains a work in progress.

Decentralized identity systems must also contend with usability and accessibility concerns. Managing cryptographic keys, verifiable credentials, and decentralized identifiers (DIDs) requires a level of technical literacy that may be challenging for non-technical users. If decentralized identity systems are too complex to use, individuals may revert to more familiar, centralized identity solutions, negating the benefits of self-sovereign identity. User-friendly interfaces, intuitive identity wallets, and clear guidance on managing digital credentials are essential to ensuring adoption by a broad user base.

Security vulnerabilities in decentralized identity implementations can also pose risks. Smart contracts, identity wallets, and cryptographic protocols used in decentralized identity systems may contain exploitable weaknesses. A vulnerability in a widely used decentralized identity platform could result in the loss or theft of identity credentials on a large scale. Ensuring the security of decentralized identity infrastructure requires continuous audits, rigorous testing, and adherence to best practices in cryptographic security.

The potential for surveillance and tracking remains a concern in decentralized identity ecosystems. While SSI is designed to enhance privacy, some implementations may inadvertently allow for transaction tracking and identity correlation. If verifiable credentials and DIDs are linked across multiple services without sufficient privacy protections, users' activities could be monitored, undermining the very principles of decentralized identity. Privacy-enhancing techniques such as zero-knowledge proofs, decentralized credential issuance, and selective disclosure must be implemented to prevent identity tracking and ensure that users retain full control over their digital footprint.

Resistance from traditional identity providers and institutions may also hinder the adoption of decentralized identity. Governments, financial institutions, and large corporations have long relied on centralized identity systems that provide them with control over user data. These entities may be reluctant to adopt decentralized identity models that reduce their influence over identity verification processes. Overcoming institutional resistance requires demonstrating the security, efficiency, and regulatory compliance of decentralized identity solutions while highlighting the benefits of user-centric identity management.

Decentralized identity offers a transformative approach to digital identity management, but it is not without risks. Addressing these risks requires collaboration between technology providers, governments, regulatory bodies, and users to develop secure, scalable, and privacy-preserving identity solutions. By implementing strong cryptographic security measures, ensuring regulatory compliance, enhancing usability, and fostering interoperability, decentralized identity systems can overcome these challenges and provide a more secure and user-controlled alternative to traditional identity models.

Decentralized Identity in Financial Services

The financial sector relies heavily on identity verification to ensure compliance with regulations, prevent fraud, and provide secure access to banking and financial services. Traditional identity systems in financial services depend on centralized databases, government-issued credentials, and third-party identity providers. While these systems have been effective in establishing trust, they introduce significant inefficiencies, privacy concerns, and security risks. Decentralized identity offers an alternative approach that enhances security, reduces reliance on intermediaries, and empowers individuals with greater control over their financial identity.

Decentralized identity in financial services is built on the principles of self-sovereign identity (SSI), where individuals own and control their digital credentials. Instead of relying on a central authority to verify identity, decentralized identity solutions use cryptographic proofs, blockchain technology, and verifiable credentials to enable secure, privacy-preserving identity verification. This model reduces dependency on centralized institutions while ensuring that identity claims remain tamper-proof and easily verifiable across multiple financial platforms.

One of the primary benefits of decentralized identity in financial services is its potential to streamline Know Your Customer (KYC) and Anti-Money Laundering (AML) compliance processes. Financial institutions are required to verify the identity of customers before offering services, a process that typically involves collecting personal documents, running background checks, and storing sensitive information in centralized databases. This approach is costly, time-consuming, and prone to security breaches. With decentralized identity, individuals can present verifiable credentials issued by trusted entities, such as governments or banks, without sharing excessive personal data. These credentials can be cryptographically verified, eliminating the need for repeated identity verification across multiple financial institutions.

Decentralized identity also enhances security and reduces fraud in financial transactions. Centralized identity databases are prime targets for cybercriminals, who exploit security vulnerabilities to steal personal data, commit identity theft, and engage in financial fraud. By removing centralized repositories of identity data, decentralized identity systems significantly reduce the risk of large-scale breaches. Each user controls their private keys and identity credentials, ensuring that identity verification occurs without exposing sensitive information to unnecessary third parties.

Privacy is another critical advantage of decentralized identity in financial services. Traditional identity verification methods often require individuals to disclose more information than necessary. For example, when proving eligibility for a financial product, users may be required to share full personal details, including their name, address, and government-issued ID number, even if only a subset of this information is relevant. Decentralized identity enables selective disclosure through cryptographic techniques such as zero-knowledge proofs (ZKPs), allowing individuals to prove specific attributes—such as age, income level, or citizenship—without revealing additional personal details. This privacy-enhancing feature ensures compliance with data protection regulations while minimizing the risk of identity exposure.

Cross-border transactions and global financial inclusion are areas where decentralized identity can have a profound impact. Many individuals, particularly in developing regions, lack access to formal banking services due to the absence of recognized identity documents. Traditional financial systems often exclude those without government-issued credentials, limiting economic opportunities for millions of people worldwide. Decentralized identity allows individuals to build and manage their own digital identities, leveraging verifiable credentials issued by trusted organizations, community networks, or decentralized reputation systems. By enabling individuals to prove their financial history, creditworthiness, or eligibility for financial services without relying on a single issuing authority, decentralized identity expands financial inclusion and provides access to banking, loans, and investment opportunities.

Financial institutions can also benefit from reduced operational costs by integrating decentralized identity solutions. Identity verification and compliance processes currently require significant resources, including manual document checks, data storage, and fraud detection systems. Decentralized identity automates these processes, allowing financial institutions to verify credentials instantly without direct interactions with issuers. This not only improves efficiency but also reduces the administrative burden on financial service providers, freeing up resources for innovation and customer experience improvements.

Decentralized identity also plays a role in enhancing secure authentication and access management for financial services. Traditional authentication methods rely on usernames, passwords, and multi-factor authentication (MFA) mechanisms, which can be susceptible to phishing attacks and credential leaks. With decentralized identity, authentication is based on cryptographic signatures rather than static credentials. Users can authenticate themselves using decentralized identifiers (DIDs) and verifiable credentials stored in digital wallets, eliminating the need for passwords while enhancing security.

The integration of decentralized identity into decentralized finance (DeFi) platforms further demonstrates its potential in transforming financial services. DeFi applications operate on blockchain networks and require secure, verifiable identity solutions to prevent fraud, ensure regulatory compliance, and enhance user trust. Decentralized identity allows users to prove their reputation, creditworthiness, and compliance status without compromising their privacy. By enabling verifiable identity claims without reliance on centralized authorities, decentralized identity solutions make DeFi platforms more secure, transparent, and accessible to a broader range of users.

Despite its advantages, the adoption of decentralized identity in financial services faces several challenges. One of the main hurdles is regulatory compliance. Financial institutions operate under strict regulatory frameworks that mandate customer identity verification, transaction monitoring, and fraud prevention. While decentralized identity aligns with privacy-focused regulations such as the General Data Protection Regulation (GDPR), it must also comply with financial industry standards for identity verification and reporting. Governments and regulatory bodies must establish guidelines that allow decentralized identity to be integrated into existing compliance frameworks without introducing new risks.

Another challenge is interoperability. Financial services operate across multiple platforms, regions, and regulatory jurisdictions. Decentralized identity solutions must be designed to work seamlessly across different financial institutions, payment networks, and identity verification providers. Efforts to establish common standards, such as those developed by the Decentralized Identity Foundation (DIF) and the World Wide Web Consortium (W3C), are essential for ensuring that decentralized identity can be used universally within financial ecosystems.

User education and adoption are also critical factors in the successful implementation of decentralized identity in financial services. Managing decentralized identity credentials requires a certain level of technical literacy, and users must understand how to secure their private keys, protect their identity wallets, and recover lost credentials. Financial institutions must provide user-friendly interfaces, clear guidance, and robust key recovery mechanisms to encourage adoption while maintaining security and usability.

The transition to decentralized identity in financial services represents a shift toward a more secure, efficient, and privacy-preserving financial ecosystem. By reducing reliance on centralized identity providers, enhancing fraud prevention, and enabling financial inclusion, decentralized identity has the potential to reshape the way identity verification and authentication are conducted in banking, payments, and digital finance. As technology matures and regulatory frameworks evolve, decentralized identity solutions will play an increasingly vital role in building a trust-based financial infrastructure that empowers individuals and businesses alike.

SSI for Healthcare and Medical Records

Self-sovereign identity (SSI) is transforming the way individuals manage their digital identities, providing more control, privacy, and security. In the healthcare sector, where sensitive personal data is frequently exchanged between patients, healthcare providers, insurance companies, and regulators, SSI presents a revolutionary approach to managing medical records. Traditional healthcare identity systems rely on centralized databases, which are vulnerable to data breaches, inefficiencies, and lack of interoperability. SSI enables individuals to control access to their health data, improving security, reducing administrative burdens, and ensuring patient privacy while maintaining compliance with regulations such as HIPAA and GDPR.

One of the primary challenges in healthcare is patient identity management. Current healthcare systems often require patients to repeatedly verify their identity at different healthcare facilities, leading to redundant data collection, delays in care, and risks of misidentification. With an SSI-based healthcare identity, patients can create and manage their own decentralized identity, which they use to authenticate themselves across various healthcare providers. This eliminates the need for multiple records in different hospital databases, reducing errors and improving the efficiency of care delivery.

Medical records are among the most sensitive types of personal information. Traditional systems store patient data in centralized repositories, often managed by hospitals, insurance providers, or government agencies. These centralized databases are prime targets for cybercriminals seeking to steal personal health information for fraud, identity theft, or black-market sale. With SSI, medical records are not stored in a single location but instead linked to verifiable credentials that are controlled by the patient. Instead of relying on a centralized system, SSI enables patients to store their medical credentials in a digital wallet, granting access only to authorized healthcare providers when needed.

A key benefit of SSI in healthcare is privacy-enhancing data sharing. Patients frequently need to share portions of their medical history with doctors, specialists, or insurance companies, but under traditional systems, they often have little control over what is shared. SSI allows for selective disclosure, meaning that a patient can provide proof of a medical condition or vaccination status without exposing their entire health record. Using cryptographic techniques such as zero-knowledge proofs (ZKPs), patients can prove they meet specific health criteria without revealing unnecessary personal details. For example, a patient seeking travel approval could prove they are vaccinated against a disease without disclosing additional medical information.

Interoperability is another major advantage of SSI for healthcare. Many healthcare institutions operate in siloed systems, making it difficult for patients and doctors to access complete medical histories across different hospitals or regions. When a patient switches doctors, hospitals, or insurance providers, their medical records often need to be transferred manually, a process that is slow and prone to errors. With SSI, medical credentials follow the patient, allowing them to instantly share accurate health data with any authorized provider. This ensures continuity of care and reduces administrative inefficiencies.

Health insurance verification and claims processing also benefit from SSI. Currently, insurance companies require extensive documentation to verify a patient's eligibility and medical history, leading to long processing times and potential errors. SSI enables insurance providers to instantly verify patient credentials and claims through cryptographic attestations, reducing paperwork and fraud while speeding up approvals and reimbursements. Patients can present verifiable credentials proving their coverage, eligibility, and prior authorizations without repeatedly submitting paperwork.

Clinical trials and medical research also require secure and compliant handling of patient data. SSI allows individuals to participate in research studies while maintaining control over their personal data. Researchers can verify a participant's eligibility through cryptographic proofs without exposing their full medical history. Additionally, SSI enables patients to grant or revoke access to their anonymized data, supporting ethical research practices while ensuring compliance with privacy regulations. This approach enhances trust between patients and medical researchers while improving the integrity of clinical studies.

SSI is also particularly beneficial for emergency healthcare situations. In cases where a patient is unconscious or unable to communicate, medical providers need instant access to critical health information, such as allergies, pre-existing conditions, or emergency contacts. With SSI, patients can store emergency medical credentials in their digital identity wallet, which authorized first responders can access quickly. This ensures that emergency care providers have accurate, up-to-date information, reducing the risk of medical errors and improving patient outcomes.

For governments and public health agencies, SSI provides a powerful tool for managing public health initiatives such as vaccination programs, disease tracking, and health certifications. During the COVID-19 pandemic, the need for verifiable health credentials became clear, as individuals were required to prove their vaccination or test status for travel and work. SSI enables governments to issue digital health credentials that citizens can store in their identity wallets and present when needed, ensuring authenticity without compromising privacy.

Despite its advantages, SSI in healthcare faces several challenges. One of the key barriers to adoption is regulatory compliance. Healthcare systems must adhere to strict regulations such as HIPAA in the United States and GDPR in Europe, which require careful handling of patient data. While SSI aligns with privacy principles by giving patients control over their data, integrating SSI with existing legal frameworks requires collaboration between regulators, healthcare providers, and technology developers. Governments and health agencies must establish clear guidelines on how SSI can be implemented in a compliant manner.

Another challenge is user adoption and accessibility. Many patients, particularly elderly individuals or those in low-resource settings, may struggle with the technical aspects of managing a digital identity wallet. Healthcare providers must ensure that SSI solutions are designed with user-friendly interfaces and provide support for individuals who may not be familiar with digital identity management.

Educational campaigns and technical assistance will be necessary to encourage widespread adoption.

Security is another consideration, as SSI systems must ensure that cryptographic keys and digital credentials are properly protected. Losing access to a digital identity wallet could result in a patient being unable to retrieve critical medical records. Backup and recovery solutions, such as multi-signature authentication or trusted contacts, must be integrated into SSI healthcare solutions to prevent identity loss.

Healthcare providers must also address integration challenges. Many hospitals and insurance companies operate on legacy systems that may not be immediately compatible with decentralized identity technologies. Transitioning to an SSI-based system requires investment in infrastructure, training for medical professionals, and collaboration with technology providers to ensure seamless integration.

Self-sovereign identity represents a transformative approach to healthcare identity management, offering greater privacy, security, and efficiency. By enabling patients to control their medical records, facilitating seamless data sharing, and reducing administrative burdens, SSI has the potential to improve healthcare delivery while ensuring compliance with privacy regulations. As adoption grows, collaboration between healthcare institutions, technology developers, and policymakers will be essential to realizing the full benefits of decentralized identity in healthcare.

Digital Identity for Education and Certifications

The education sector relies on identity verification and credentialing systems to authenticate students, verify academic achievements, and issue certifications. Traditionally, these processes are managed by centralized institutions such as universities, certification bodies, and government agencies. However, this centralized approach presents challenges such as credential fraud, inefficiencies in verification, and limited user control over academic records. Digital identity, particularly self-sovereign identity (SSI), offers a transformative approach to managing education credentials, allowing students to securely store, control, and share their achievements in a decentralized and verifiable manner.

One of the primary challenges in education is credential verification. Universities and certification bodies issue degrees, diplomas, and professional certifications, but verifying these credentials often requires manual checks, institutional involvement, and time-consuming processes. Employers, educational institutions, and government agencies must contact issuing organizations to confirm the authenticity of a candidate's academic record. This process is inefficient, prone to errors, and susceptible to credential fraud. Digital identity solutions, using verifiable credentials (VCs) and decentralized identifiers (DIDs), allow educational institutions to issue cryptographically signed academic records that can be instantly verified without needing to contact the issuer.

With digital identity, students receive verifiable credentials upon completing courses, degrees, or certifications. These credentials are stored in a digital identity wallet controlled by the student. Instead of requesting transcripts or certificates from multiple institutions, students can share their credentials directly with employers, universities, or licensing boards. The recipients can verify the authenticity of these credentials using cryptographic proofs, ensuring that the documents have not been tampered with and are issued by a legitimate institution. This significantly reduces administrative burdens while enhancing trust in the credentialing system.

Another significant benefit of digital identity in education is the prevention of diploma and certification fraud. Fake degrees and fraudulent certifications are a widespread issue, affecting hiring decisions, professional licensing, and the credibility of academic institutions. Because verifiable credentials are cryptographically signed and anchored on decentralized networks, they cannot be forged or altered. This ensures that only legitimate degree holders can claim academic qualifications, strengthening the integrity of academic and professional credentials.

Interoperability is a critical aspect of digital identity for education. Students often earn credentials from multiple sources, including universities, online learning platforms, professional training programs, and industry certifications. Traditional systems require students to manage separate records for each institution, making it difficult to consolidate and share their full academic and professional achievements. Digital identity solutions enable interoperability by adhering to open standards such as those developed by the World Wide Web Consortium (W3C) and the Decentralized Identity Foundation (DIF). These standards ensure that verifiable credentials issued by different organizations are compatible and can be used across multiple platforms, institutions, and industries.

Lifelong learning is becoming increasingly important in today's workforce, where individuals continuously acquire new skills and certifications throughout their careers. Digital identity supports lifelong learning by allowing individuals to accumulate and manage credentials over time. Whether it's a university degree, a coding bootcamp certificate, or a professional development course, all credentials can be stored in a single digital wallet, providing a comprehensive and verifiable record of a person's academic and professional journey. This empowers individuals with greater control over their qualifications and makes career transitions more seamless.

For employers, digital identity simplifies the hiring process by providing instant verification of a candidate's educational background. Traditional background checks can take days or even weeks, often requiring employers to contact multiple institutions to validate degrees and certifications. With verifiable credentials, employers can verify a candidate's qualifications instantly, reducing hiring time and improving efficiency. Additionally, digital identity eliminates the risk of falsified credentials, ensuring that hiring decisions are based on accurate and verified information.

Government agencies and licensing bodies can also benefit from digital identity in education. Many professions require licensing and continuous education to maintain credentials. Using verifiable credentials, licensing bodies can streamline the process of verifying a professional's qualifications, ensuring compliance with regulatory requirements. Healthcare professionals, lawyers, engineers, and other licensed professionals can use digital identity wallets to store and present their credentials whenever required, simplifying renewals and regulatory checks.

Digital identity solutions also enhance accessibility and inclusion in education. Millions of people worldwide lack access to traditional identity documents, making it difficult for them to enroll in educational programs or verify their qualifications. Refugees, displaced individuals, and those in underserved regions often struggle to access higher education or employment opportunities due to missing or lost documents. Digital identity allows individuals to create and maintain portable, verifiable records of their education history, even if they move across borders or lose access to original documents. This can significantly improve access to education and career opportunities for marginalized populations.

Despite its advantages, implementing digital identity in education comes with challenges. One of the primary concerns is ensuring that digital identity solutions comply with data protection regulations such as the General Data Protection Regulation (GDPR) in Europe. While decentralized identity systems enhance privacy by allowing users to control their credentials, institutions must ensure that personal data is handled securely and that students retain full control over how their credentials are shared.

Another challenge is the adoption of digital identity by educational institutions and employers. Many universities and organizations still rely on traditional paper-based credentialing systems, and transitioning to a digital model requires investment in infrastructure, training, and policy development. Institutions must collaborate with technology providers, regulatory bodies, and industry stakeholders to establish best practices for digital identity implementation.

Usability is also a key factor in the success of digital identity in education. Managing digital credentials should be simple and intuitive for students, faculty, and employers. User-friendly digital wallets, clear authentication processes, and seamless integration with existing academic platforms are essential to ensuring widespread adoption. If digital identity solutions are too complex, users may be hesitant to adopt them, limiting their effectiveness.

The shift toward digital identity in education represents a major advancement in how academic credentials are issued, stored, and verified. By leveraging decentralized technologies, cryptographic verification, and interoperability standards, digital identity enhances security, reduces fraud, and provides individuals with greater control over their academic and professional records. As educational institutions, governments, and industries recognize the benefits of self-sovereign identity, digital identity solutions will become increasingly integrated into the global education and certification ecosystem.

Identity in Supply Chain and Logistics

The supply chain and logistics industry relies on trust, transparency, and efficiency to ensure that goods move securely across different regions, suppliers, and stakeholders. Identity verification plays a critical role in managing suppliers, verifying product authenticity, tracking shipments, and ensuring compliance with regulatory standards. However, traditional identity management systems in supply chains are often fragmented, relying on centralized databases, manual record-keeping, and intermediary-based verification processes. This leads to inefficiencies, increased costs, fraud risks, and delays.

Digital identity solutions, particularly decentralized identity frameworks, offer a more secure and streamlined approach to managing identities within supply chain networks. By leveraging self-sovereign identity (SSI) principles, decentralized identifiers (DIDs), and verifiable credentials (VCs), businesses can improve traceability, enhance security, and reduce administrative burdens. This shift towards digital identity not only improves efficiency but also strengthens trust among supply chain participants.

One of the primary challenges in supply chain identity management is the verification of suppliers and vendors. In global supply chains, companies interact with multiple suppliers, manufacturers, and logistics providers, each operating under different standards and regulations. Traditional supplier onboarding processes require extensive documentation, background checks, and manual verification, which can be time-consuming and prone to errors. Digital identity enables suppliers to create verifiable credentials that prove their legitimacy, compliance, and certifications without requiring repeated manual verification. Businesses can instantly verify a supplier's credentials using cryptographic signatures, ensuring authenticity and reducing the risk of fraud.

Product authentication and anti-counterfeiting measures also benefit from digital identity solutions. Counterfeit goods pose a significant risk in industries such as pharmaceuticals, electronics, and luxury goods. Traditional methods of verifying product authenticity rely on physical labels, barcodes, or paper-based certificates, which can be easily manipulated or forged. By using decentralized identity and blockchain-based traceability, manufacturers can issue verifiable credentials for each product batch, linking them to a digital identity that certifies their authenticity. This allows retailers, regulators, and consumers to verify a product's origin and legitimacy instantly, reducing the risk of counterfeit infiltration in the supply chain.

Logistics companies also face challenges related to shipment tracking and cargo integrity. Many supply chain networks use centralized tracking systems that lack real-time visibility and interoperability. Decentralized identity solutions enable unique digital identities for shipments, allowing stakeholders to verify and track goods securely. Each shipment can be assigned a decentralized identifier (DID) linked to verifiable credentials that document its origin, transit history, and handling conditions. This enhances transparency, reduces disputes, and ensures compliance with regulatory requirements.

Regulatory compliance and auditability are crucial aspects of supply chain management, particularly in industries with strict regulations such as food safety, pharmaceuticals, and hazardous materials. Companies must maintain detailed records of product handling, storage conditions, and regulatory certifications. Traditional compliance reporting involves extensive paperwork and manual audits, increasing operational costs and inefficiencies. Digital identity solutions allow businesses to generate and store verifiable credentials that prove compliance with regulations, making audits faster and more efficient. Regulators and auditors can verify compliance records instantly without needing direct access to proprietary databases, ensuring a secure and tamper-proof compliance framework.

The transportation and logistics sector also faces identity verification challenges related to drivers, warehouse personnel, and cross-border shipments. Truck drivers, port workers, and logistics operators must present identification credentials at various checkpoints, leading to delays and inefficiencies. Digital identity enables workers to store verifiable credentials in digital wallets, allowing for quick identity verification without relying on paper documents. This approach improves security, reduces identity fraud, and speeds up logistics operations at borders, warehouses, and distribution centers.

Cross-border trade presents additional complexities, as different countries have varying customs regulations, documentation requirements, and trade compliance rules. Traditional customs clearance processes involve multiple intermediaries, leading to delays and additional costs. Decentralized identity solutions facilitate cross-border trade by enabling secure identity verification for importers, exporters, and customs authorities. With verifiable credentials, businesses can present digital trade documents, reducing paperwork and expediting customs processing. This streamlining of trade compliance improves efficiency while maintaining security and regulatory adherence.

Sustainability and ethical sourcing are becoming increasingly important in supply chain management. Consumers and regulators demand greater transparency regarding the origins of raw materials, labor practices, and environmental impact. Digital identity solutions allow businesses to create verified records of sustainability certifications, fair labor practices, and responsible sourcing initiatives. By issuing verifiable credentials for ethical sourcing certifications, companies can provide customers with proof of compliance, strengthening consumer trust and brand reputation.

Despite the advantages of digital identity in supply chain and logistics, there are challenges to widespread adoption. One of the main concerns is interoperability among different supply chain stakeholders. Many companies operate on proprietary systems that may not be compatible with decentralized identity frameworks. Efforts to establish open standards, such as those developed by the Decentralized Identity Foundation (DIF) and the World Wide Web Consortium (W3C), are critical to ensuring seamless integration across supply chain networks.

Another challenge is data privacy and security. While digital identity enhances security, businesses must ensure that sensitive supplier, shipment, and trade data remain protected. Implementing privacy-preserving technologies such as zero-knowledge proofs (ZKPs) allows companies to verify supply chain credentials without exposing confidential business information. These techniques enable secure identity verification while maintaining compliance with data protection regulations such as GDPR.

Adoption barriers also exist due to the need for education and infrastructure investment. Many supply chain participants, particularly small and medium-sized enterprises (SMEs), may lack the technical knowledge or resources to implement digital identity solutions. Governments, industry groups, and technology providers must collaborate to offer training, financial support, and scalable identity frameworks that accommodate businesses of all sizes.

The role of government and regulatory bodies is also crucial in shaping the adoption of decentralized identity in supply chains. Governments can support digital identity initiatives by establishing legal frameworks for verifiable credentials, encouraging interoperability, and integrating digital identity into trade policies. Public-private partnerships can facilitate pilot programs and real-world implementations that demonstrate the benefits of decentralized identity in logistics and supply chain operations.

Digital identity is transforming supply chain and logistics by enhancing security, efficiency, and transparency. By enabling verifiable supplier credentials, product authentication, secure shipment tracking, regulatory compliance, and cross-border trade facilitation, decentralized identity solutions reduce fraud, streamline operations, and improve trust among stakeholders. As technology evolves and adoption increases, digital identity will become a fundamental component of modern supply chain management, driving efficiency, security, and sustainability across global trade networks.

The Future of Digital Identity in E-Government

As governments worldwide shift toward digital transformation, e-government services are becoming increasingly essential for delivering public services efficiently and securely. Digital identity plays a foundational role in e-government, enabling citizens to authenticate themselves, access government resources, and interact with public institutions online. Traditional government-issued digital identities, such as national ID cards, social security numbers, and passport systems, often rely on centralized models. While these systems provide structured identity management, they also present challenges such as security vulnerabilities, identity theft, and limited user control.

The evolution of digital identity in e-government is moving toward decentralized and self-sovereign identity (SSI) models. These approaches enhance security, privacy, and accessibility while reducing dependency on centralized databases. By leveraging decentralized identifiers (DIDs), verifiable credentials (VCs), and blockchain-based authentication, governments can create a more user-centric identity framework that allows citizens to own and control their digital identities. This transformation ensures that digital government services are more efficient, secure, and inclusive.

One of the primary drivers of digital identity in e-government is the need for secure and seamless authentication. Governments require robust identity verification mechanisms to deliver services such as tax filing, social security benefits, voting, healthcare access, and business registrations. Traditional username-password authentication systems are vulnerable to phishing attacks, credential theft, and fraud. Digital identity solutions based on cryptographic authentication, including biometrics and decentralized identity verification, reduce these risks by providing stronger authentication mechanisms without relying on static credentials.

Privacy and data protection are critical concerns in e-government identity systems. Many traditional government identity solutions store personal data in centralized databases, making them attractive targets for cyberattacks. Data breaches involving government records can expose millions of citizens to identity fraud, financial theft, and unauthorized surveillance. Decentralized identity models mitigate these risks by allowing individuals to store their credentials in digital wallets rather than centralized repositories. With selective disclosure techniques, such as zero-knowledge proofs (ZKPs), citizens can verify attributes like age, residency, or eligibility for government programs without revealing excessive personal information.

Interoperability is another key challenge in digital identity for e-government. Citizens interact with multiple government agencies that operate under different identity verification frameworks. In many cases, individuals must create separate accounts for different services, leading to redundant identity verification processes and inefficient service delivery. A unified digital identity system enables citizens to use a single, verifiable identity across various government agencies and services. By adopting open standards such as those developed by the World Wide Web Consortium (W3C) and the Decentralized Identity Foundation (DIF), governments can ensure that digital identities are portable, interoperable, and compatible across different sectors.

E-government services also benefit from the automation and efficiency gains provided by digital identity. Many bureaucratic processes require extensive paperwork, manual verification, and in-person authentication. Digital identity streamlines these workflows by enabling instant identity verification, reducing administrative costs, and minimizing processing times. Citizens can digitally sign documents, submit applications, and receive government benefits without needing to visit physical offices. Smart contracts and blockchain-based identity verification further enhance automation by enabling self-executing agreements and secure digital transactions.

Digital identity plays a crucial role in strengthening e-voting systems, ensuring election integrity and accessibility. Traditional voting systems, whether paper-based or electronic, face challenges related to voter authentication, fraud prevention, and transparency. With decentralized identity, governments can implement secure digital voting platforms where citizens can verify their eligibility and cast votes without compromising privacy. Verifiable credentials ensure that only eligible voters participate, while blockchain-based ledgers provide an immutable record of votes to enhance trust in electoral processes.

Social welfare programs and public benefits distribution are areas where digital identity significantly improves efficiency and reduces fraud. Governments often struggle with ensuring that benefits reach the right individuals while preventing fraud and duplicate claims. Traditional welfare systems require extensive identity verification and manual approvals, leading to delays and inefficiencies. With digital identity, eligible citizens can present verifiable credentials that prove their eligibility for social programs, reducing paperwork and enabling faster disbursement of benefits. Automated identity verification also minimizes fraudulent claims by ensuring that only verified individuals receive assistance.

The integration of digital identity with financial inclusion initiatives is another important aspect of e-government services. Many citizens, particularly those in developing regions, lack formal identification, limiting their access to banking services, loans, and financial aid. Governments can issue digital identity credentials that serve as proof of identity, enabling individuals to open bank accounts, receive digital payments, and participate in economic activities. Decentralized identity solutions further enhance financial inclusion by allowing individuals to build portable financial histories based on verifiable credentials rather than relying solely on traditional credit bureaus.

Cross-border digital identity recognition is a growing priority for governments, especially in regions with high levels of migration and international trade. Many individuals face challenges in proving their identity when moving between countries, applying for work permits, or accessing government services abroad. By adopting decentralized identity frameworks, governments can facilitate cross-border identity verification while preserving privacy and sovereignty. Initiatives such as the European Blockchain Services Infrastructure (EBSI) are exploring ways to create interoperable digital identity solutions that allow citizens to use their credentials internationally.

Despite the advantages of digital identity in e-government, several challenges must be addressed for widespread adoption. Regulatory frameworks must evolve to accommodate decentralized identity models while maintaining compliance with data protection laws such as the General Data Protection Regulation (GDPR) and national cybersecurity policies. Governments must establish legal recognition for digital credentials and verifiable identity claims, ensuring that they hold the same legitimacy as traditional identity documents.

User adoption and digital literacy are also critical factors. Many citizens, particularly older populations and those in rural areas, may not be familiar with digital identity concepts. Governments must invest in public education initiatives, user-friendly identity wallets, and accessible digital platforms to ensure that digital identity solutions are inclusive and easy to use. Simplified identity recovery mechanisms must also be implemented to prevent individuals from losing access to their digital credentials due to lost devices or forgotten authentication keys.

The future of digital identity in e-government will be shaped by technological advancements, regulatory developments, and public-private collaboration. Governments must work closely with technology providers, identity standards organizations, and civil society groups to develop identity systems that balance security, privacy, and usability. By adopting decentralized, interoperable, and privacy-preserving digital identity frameworks, governments can create a more efficient, secure, and citizen-centric e-government infrastructure.

Privacy-Preserving Identity Solutions

The digital age has brought significant advancements in identity management, enabling individuals and organizations to verify identities online more efficiently. However, the widespread use of digital identity systems has also raised concerns about privacy, data security, and user control over personal information. Traditional identity verification methods often require individuals to share excessive amounts of personal data with third parties, increasing the risks of identity theft, data breaches, and unauthorized surveillance. Privacy-preserving identity solutions offer an alternative approach by leveraging cryptographic techniques and decentralized identity frameworks to ensure that identity verification is both secure and privacy-respecting.

A fundamental principle of privacy-preserving identity solutions is minimizing data exposure. In traditional identity systems, when a user needs to prove their age, they typically present a government-issued ID that reveals not only their date of birth but also their full name, address, and other personal details. This excessive data exposure creates unnecessary privacy risks. Privacy-preserving identity solutions address this issue by using selective disclosure mechanisms that allow users to verify specific attributes without revealing unrelated information. Cryptographic techniques such as zero-knowledge proofs (ZKPs) enable users to prove statements—such as being over 18—without exposing their exact birth date.

Self-sovereign identity (SSI) plays a crucial role in privacy-preserving identity solutions by giving users complete control over their digital credentials. Instead of relying on centralized identity providers that store user data in large databases, SSI allows individuals to manage their credentials in digital wallets. Users can present verifiable credentials issued by trusted entities, such as governments or educational institutions, while maintaining control over when and how their data is shared. This decentralized model eliminates the need for intermediaries and reduces the risk of mass data breaches.

Decentralized identifiers (DIDs) are a key component of privacy-preserving identity solutions. Unlike traditional identifiers, such as email addresses or social security numbers, DIDs are user-generated and not tied to any central authority. Each DID is linked to cryptographic keys that allow users to authenticate themselves without relying on passwords or third-party verification services. This approach enhances privacy by ensuring that individuals can interact with digital services without creating a trail of personally identifiable information (PII) that can be exploited for tracking or surveillance.

Verifiable credentials (VCs) further enhance privacy by enabling users to prove their identity or qualifications without exposing raw personal data. For example, an employer verifying a job candidate's educational background does not need to access the candidate's entire academic record. Instead, the candidate can present a verifiable credential confirming their degree, signed by the issuing university, which the employer can verify instantly. Because these credentials are cryptographically signed and tamper-proof, they eliminate the need for manual verification while ensuring authenticity and privacy.

Another critical aspect of privacy-preserving identity solutions is the use of zero-knowledge proofs (ZKPs). ZKPs are cryptographic protocols that allow one party to prove knowledge of certain information without revealing the actual data. This technique is particularly useful in identity verification scenarios where individuals need to prove attributes, such as citizenship or income level, without exposing sensitive details. ZKPs are being integrated into various identity frameworks to enhance privacy in financial transactions, healthcare access, and online authentication.

Privacy-enhancing authentication methods are also gaining traction as part of privacy-preserving identity solutions. Traditional authentication relies on usernames, passwords, and multi-factor authentication (MFA), which often require users to share personal information with service providers. Privacy-preserving authentication techniques, such as anonymous credentials and decentralized authentication protocols, allow users to authenticate themselves without disclosing unnecessary details. One example is the use of cryptographic attestations, where a trusted entity signs a user's authentication request without revealing their identity to the service provider.

Blockchain technology plays a role in privacy-preserving identity solutions by providing a decentralized and tamper-resistant way to verify credentials without relying on centralized databases. However, storing personal identity data directly on the blockchain poses privacy risks, as blockchain records are immutable and publicly accessible. To address this challenge, privacy-preserving identity solutions use off-chain storage for sensitive data while anchoring cryptographic proofs on the blockchain. This hybrid approach ensures that verifications are secure and auditable without exposing personal information.

Regulatory compliance is an essential consideration for privacy-preserving identity solutions. Governments and regulatory bodies impose strict data protection laws, such as the General Data Protection Regulation (GDPR) in Europe, which mandate that organizations minimize data collection, ensure user consent, and provide mechanisms for data portability. Privacy-preserving identity frameworks align with these regulations by enabling individuals to control their own data, reducing the need for unnecessary data retention, and ensuring that identity verification processes are transparent and auditable.

One of the key challenges in implementing privacy-preserving identity solutions is user adoption and ease of use. Many individuals are unfamiliar with cryptographic concepts and may find managing decentralized identity wallets complex. Ensuring that privacy-preserving identity systems are user-friendly, intuitive, and accessible to people with varying levels of digital literacy is crucial for widespread adoption. Solutions such as biometric authentication, intuitive mobile applications, and simple key recovery mechanisms can help bridge the gap between advanced cryptographic security and everyday usability.

Another challenge is interoperability between different identity ecosystems. Various organizations, governments, and technology providers are developing their own decentralized identity frameworks, each with unique technical implementations. To enable seamless identity verification across multiple platforms, interoperability standards must be established. Initiatives such as the Decentralized Identity Foundation (DIF) and the World Wide Web Consortium (W3C) are working on global identity standards that allow different identity systems to communicate securely while preserving user privacy.

Financial institutions, healthcare providers, and government agencies are among the key adopters of privacy-preserving identity solutions. In financial services, these solutions enable privacy-enhanced KYC (Know Your Customer) and AML (Anti-Money Laundering) compliance, allowing banks to verify customer identities without storing excessive personal data. In healthcare, privacy-preserving identity solutions allow patients to share verified medical records with doctors without exposing their full medical history. In e-government services, privacy-preserving digital identities allow citizens to access public services securely while ensuring compliance with privacy regulations.

As the demand for secure and privacy-centric digital interactions continues to grow, privacy-preserving identity solutions will play an increasingly vital role in protecting user data while enabling seamless verification. By leveraging decentralized identity frameworks, cryptographic authentication, and privacy-enhancing technologies, these solutions offer a way to balance security, compliance, and user control in the evolving digital landscape. Ensuring that privacy-preserving identity solutions are accessible, interoperable, and aligned with regulatory frameworks will be key to their successful adoption across industries.

Ethical Challenges in Decentralized Identity

Decentralized identity presents a transformative shift in how individuals manage and control their personal information. By reducing reliance on centralized authorities and enabling self-sovereign identity (SSI), decentralized identity frameworks enhance privacy, security, and user autonomy. However, despite these benefits, decentralized identity systems also introduce ethical challenges that must be carefully considered. These challenges range from accessibility and inclusion to privacy concerns, potential misuse, regulatory uncertainty, and the unintended consequences of decentralizing trust.

One of the primary ethical concerns in decentralized identity is accessibility and inclusion. While decentralized identity aims to empower individuals by giving them control over their credentials, the technology behind it requires access to digital infrastructure, internet connectivity, and a basic understanding of cryptographic key management. Many people, particularly those in developing regions or marginalized communities, may lack the necessary resources or technical literacy to manage their digital identity securely. If decentralized identity solutions are not designed with inclusivity in mind, they risk exacerbating digital divides and excluding individuals who are already underserved by traditional identity systems. Ensuring that decentralized identity is accessible to all populations requires designing user-friendly interfaces, providing educational resources, and considering alternative authentication mechanisms for those who may not have access to smartphones or internet services.

Privacy is another ethical challenge in decentralized identity. While SSI enhances privacy by allowing users to control their credentials and selectively disclose information, the implementation of decentralized identity solutions can still pose risks. The use of blockchain or distributed ledgers for identity verification raises concerns about data permanence and the potential for identity correlation. Even if personal data is not stored directly on a blockchain, transaction patterns and cryptographic proofs could be analyzed to infer personal relationships, behaviors, or financial activities. Privacy-enhancing technologies such as zero-knowledge proofs (ZKPs) and decentralized storage solutions must be integrated to ensure that decentralized identity does not become a tool for unintended surveillance or tracking.

The ethical implications of identity revocation and recovery also require careful consideration. In centralized identity systems, institutions such as governments or corporations provide mechanisms for account recovery or credential revocation. In a decentralized identity system, where individuals hold their own cryptographic keys, the loss of private keys could result in the permanent loss of access to critical services, financial accounts, or legal identities. This raises ethical concerns about whether individuals should be solely responsible for safeguarding their digital identity or if alternative recovery methods should be established. Implementing decentralized recovery solutions, such as social recovery mechanisms where trusted individuals assist in identity restoration, can help mitigate this risk, but it also introduces questions about trust delegation and potential abuse of recovery privileges.

Another ethical challenge in decentralized identity is the risk of identity misuse and fraud. While decentralized identity aims to reduce fraud by providing cryptographically verifiable credentials, bad actors could still exploit the system. For example, malicious entities could issue fraudulent credentials that appear legitimate, leading to trust manipulation and credential forgery. Decentralized identity frameworks must include mechanisms for trust verification, credential revocation, and dispute resolution to prevent the proliferation of false identities. The lack of a central authority to oversee identity validation creates an ethical dilemma regarding who should be responsible for maintaining the integrity of identity verification processes.

Regulatory uncertainty and legal recognition present additional ethical concerns. Many governments and institutions rely on established legal frameworks for identity management, but decentralized identity systems challenge these traditional models by removing centralized control. This creates friction between regulatory requirements, such as Know Your Customer (KYC) and Anti-Money Laundering (AML) laws, and the privacy-centric nature of decentralized identity. Governments may seek to impose stricter regulations on decentralized identity systems, potentially limiting their ability to function as self-sovereign solutions. Balancing the need for compliance with regulatory frameworks while preserving individual autonomy is a complex ethical challenge that requires collaboration between policymakers, identity providers, and privacy advocates.

The potential for discrimination and exclusion in decentralized identity systems also raises ethical concerns. Identity verification processes often require proof of legal existence, such as birth certificates, national IDs, or social security numbers. However, millions of people worldwide lack official identity documents due to displacement, statelessness, or systemic barriers. If decentralized identity solutions mirror traditional verification models, they may inadvertently exclude those who cannot obtain the required credentials. Ethical decentralized identity solutions should explore alternative verification methods, such as community attestations or reputation-based identity models, to ensure that individuals without formal identity documentation can still participate in digital and financial ecosystems.

Another ethical dilemma arises in the context of governance and accountability. Decentralized identity removes the need for a single authority to control identity systems, but this also means that there is no central entity responsible for addressing disputes, resolving conflicts, or enforcing ethical standards. Decentralized governance models, such as decentralized autonomous organizations (DAOs) or federated trust frameworks, attempt to address this challenge by distributing decision-making among network participants. However, ensuring fairness, preventing corruption, and establishing accountability mechanisms remain significant challenges. If governance structures are not designed carefully, decentralized identity systems could become vulnerable to power concentration among a few influential entities, contradicting their core principle of decentralization.

The ethical implications of biometric authentication within decentralized identity systems also require scrutiny. Biometrics, such as fingerprint recognition, facial scans, and voice authentication, are increasingly being used for identity verification. While biometrics enhance security, they also raise concerns about data privacy, consent, and potential misuse. Unlike passwords, biometric data cannot be changed once compromised, making it a permanent vulnerability if leaked. Furthermore, the use of biometric verification in decentralized identity systems must be designed to avoid bias and discrimination, as facial recognition technologies have been shown to exhibit racial and gender biases. Ethical implementation of biometrics requires privacy-preserving techniques such as decentralized storage, homomorphic encryption, and user-controlled biometric templates.

Decentralized identity also introduces challenges related to coercion and abuse. While self-sovereign identity is designed to empower individuals, there is a risk that governments, employers, or corporations could force individuals to share their credentials in ways that compromise their privacy or autonomy. For example, an employer could require employees to share detailed work history credentials that include personal data unrelated to job qualifications. Decentralized identity frameworks must establish clear guidelines on user consent, data minimization, and ethical credential verification to prevent coercion and misuse.

Addressing these ethical challenges requires a multi-stakeholder approach that involves technologists, policymakers, civil rights organizations, and user communities. Ethical decentralized identity systems must be designed with inclusivity, privacy, security, and accountability in mind. As decentralized identity adoption grows, ongoing discussions around ethics, governance, and user rights will be essential in shaping a fair and equitable identity ecosystem that benefits all individuals while protecting against potential harms.

Data Ownership and User Control

In the digital age, data has become one of the most valuable assets, fueling industries, shaping economies, and influencing individual lives. However, traditional digital identity systems are largely based on centralized models where corporations, governments, and service providers control and manage user data. This centralized approach often leads to security breaches, privacy concerns, and a lack of transparency in how personal information is collected, stored, and shared. The rise of decentralized identity and self-sovereign identity (SSI) models is shifting the paradigm toward data ownership and user control, empowering individuals with the ability to manage and share their personal data securely and selectively.

One of the fundamental principles of data ownership is that individuals should have full control over their personal information. In traditional identity management systems, when users sign up for online services, they are often required to provide personal details such as their name, email address, phone number, and even sensitive documents. These details are stored in centralized databases, where service providers have control over how the data is used. This creates significant risks, including unauthorized access, data breaches, and misuse of information for targeted advertising or surveillance. Decentralized identity models aim to eliminate these risks by allowing users to store their credentials in digital wallets that they control, rather than relying on a third-party provider to manage their identity.

A key component of user control is consent-based data sharing. In conventional digital interactions, users often have little choice over what data they share and how it is used. Many online services operate under opaque privacy policies, requiring users to agree to broad data collection practices without providing clear options for consent management. With decentralized identity, individuals have the ability to grant or revoke access to their personal information on a case-by-case basis. Using cryptographic techniques, such as verifiable credentials and decentralized identifiers (DIDs), users can authenticate themselves without exposing unnecessary personal details. For example, instead of sharing an entire government-issued ID to verify their age, a user can provide cryptographic proof that they meet the age requirement without revealing their birthdate or other personal information.

Data portability is another crucial aspect of data ownership. Under centralized models, user data is often locked within platforms, making it difficult to transfer or reuse across different services. Social media platforms, financial institutions, and government agencies each maintain separate identity records, forcing users to repeatedly provide the same information to different organizations. Decentralized identity enables users to carry their credentials across multiple platforms and services without needing to create redundant accounts or share excessive data. This reduces friction in digital interactions while ensuring that users retain full control over their credentials.

The security implications of data ownership and user control are also significant. Centralized identity repositories are attractive targets for cybercriminals, who exploit security vulnerabilities to steal personal data for fraud, identity theft, and financial crimes. Decentralized identity minimizes these risks by eliminating the need for large-scale data storage in centralized databases. Instead, identity credentials remain with the user, secured through encryption and private key authentication. Because decentralized identity systems do not rely on a single point of failure, they are inherently more resilient to hacking attempts and data breaches.

Another important consideration in data ownership is the right to be forgotten. In traditional digital identity systems, once personal data is shared with a service provider, it is often difficult or impossible to erase. Even if a user deletes their account, the service provider may retain records for legal, commercial, or analytical purposes. Decentralized identity gives users greater control over data retention, allowing them to revoke access to credentials and remove personal information from digital interactions. This aligns with global privacy regulations such as the General Data Protection Regulation (GDPR), which grants individuals the right to request the deletion of their personal data.

Despite its advantages, decentralized identity and data ownership present challenges in key management and accessibility. Unlike traditional identity systems, where users can reset passwords or recover accounts through customer support, decentralized identity relies on cryptographic keys that must be securely stored. Losing access to a private key can result in the permanent loss of an individual's digital identity, making it difficult to regain access to online services. To address this challenge, decentralized identity solutions incorporate backup mechanisms such as multi-signature authentication, social recovery, and secure key storage options that balance security with usability.

Regulatory and legal considerations also play a role in the evolution of data ownership. Governments and regulatory bodies are still adapting to decentralized identity frameworks, and legal recognition of self-sovereign identity credentials varies by jurisdiction. While some countries are exploring blockchain-based identity systems to enhance security and efficiency in government services, others remain cautious about the implications of fully decentralized identity models. Ensuring compliance with legal frameworks while preserving individual control over data is a delicate balance that requires collaboration between policymakers, technology developers, and civil rights organizations.

User adoption and education are additional challenges in the widespread adoption of data ownership and decentralized identity. Many individuals are accustomed to centralized identity models and may be hesitant to transition to a system where they bear full responsibility for managing their credentials. To encourage adoption, decentralized identity solutions must offer intuitive user experiences, seamless authentication processes, and accessible recovery mechanisms. Public awareness campaigns and educational initiatives can also help users understand the benefits of data ownership and the importance of controlling their digital identity.

The role of decentralized identity in financial services, healthcare, and e-government further illustrates the impact of data ownership. In banking, decentralized identity can streamline Know Your Customer (KYC) verification while reducing privacy risks. In healthcare, patients can manage their medical records securely, granting access only to authorized healthcare providers. In e-government services, individuals can authenticate themselves for public benefits and digital voting without relying on centralized databases. These real-world applications highlight the potential of data ownership to improve security, efficiency, and user autonomy across multiple sectors.

As digital identity systems continue to evolve, the concept of data ownership and user control will play a central role in shaping the future of online interactions. By shifting control away from centralized entities and toward individuals, decentralized identity solutions offer a privacy-preserving, secure, and user-centric approach to identity management. However, overcoming challenges related to security, legal recognition, and user adoption will require ongoing collaboration between governments, businesses, and technology providers. The future of digital identity depends on creating systems that empower individuals while ensuring interoperability, security, and trust in the digital world.

Managing Identity Fraud in a Decentralized Ecosystem

Identity fraud has long been a significant challenge in both physical and digital environments, leading to financial losses, security breaches, and privacy violations. Traditional identity systems, which rely on centralized databases and third-party verification, are particularly vulnerable to fraud due to single points of failure. When centralized identity providers are compromised, attackers can access vast amounts of personal data, enabling large-scale identity theft and fraud. Decentralized identity solutions, particularly those based on self-sovereign identity (SSI) and blockchain technology, aim to reduce these risks by eliminating central repositories of personal information. However, while decentralization enhances security and user control, it also introduces new challenges in detecting, preventing, and managing identity fraud.

One of the main challenges in managing identity fraud in a decentralized ecosystem is the lack of centralized oversight. In traditional identity systems, financial institutions, governments, and regulatory bodies monitor transactions, enforce compliance, and investigate fraudulent activities. In a decentralized identity model, individuals control their own credentials, and there is no central authority to flag suspicious behavior or revoke fraudulent identities. This creates a dilemma: how to prevent identity fraud while maintaining the principles of decentralization and user sovereignty.

Fraud prevention in decentralized identity systems relies heavily on cryptographic security and trust frameworks. Verifiable credentials (VCs) play a key role in ensuring that digital identities are legitimate and cannot be forged. Unlike traditional identity documents, which can be physically altered or counterfeited, verifiable credentials are cryptographically signed by trusted issuers. These credentials can be instantly verified using public-key cryptography, ensuring that they have not been tampered with or misrepresented. By adopting verifiable credentials, decentralized identity systems significantly reduce the risk of identity forgery.

Decentralized identifiers (DIDs) also contribute to fraud prevention by allowing individuals to create unique, self-controlled digital identities. Unlike email addresses or usernames, which can be easily duplicated or hijacked, DIDs are cryptographically secured and linked to private keys controlled by the user. This prevents identity theft by ensuring that only the legitimate identity holder can prove ownership of their credentials. However, if an individual loses access to their private key, they may be unable to recover their identity, raising concerns about key management and recovery mechanisms.

One of the emerging threats in decentralized identity systems is the creation of synthetic identities. In traditional systems, identity fraud often involves stealing or forging real credentials. In contrast, synthetic identity fraud involves creating entirely new digital personas using fabricated credentials. Attackers can use a combination of real and fake data to generate seemingly legitimate identities that pass verification checks. Because decentralized identity systems prioritize user control and privacy, it can be challenging to detect synthetic identities without centralized fraud detection mechanisms.

To mitigate the risk of synthetic identity fraud, decentralized identity ecosystems must incorporate robust identity proofing processes. Identity proofing refers to the initial verification of an individual's identity before credentials are issued. In traditional systems, this is often done through in-person verification, document checks, and biometric authentication. In a decentralized model, identity proofing can be conducted using a combination of verifiable credentials issued by trusted entities, biometric verification, and decentralized reputation systems. By establishing trust anchors—such as governments, financial institutions, and educational institutions—decentralized identity networks can ensure that only legitimate identities are created and used.

Reputation-based identity verification is another approach to managing fraud in decentralized ecosystems. In traditional credit scoring systems, an individual's financial behavior is assessed based on transaction history, credit utilization, and payment patterns. Similarly, decentralized identity systems can incorporate reputation-based verification, where an individual's trustworthiness is established through verifiable interactions. For example, a user who has consistently used verifiable credentials from multiple trusted issuers—such as banks, employers, and educational institutions—can build a strong reputation over time. This reputation can serve as an additional layer of fraud prevention, making it more difficult for fraudulent identities to gain legitimacy.

Decentralized identity systems can also leverage artificial intelligence (AI) and machine learning (ML) to detect fraudulent activities. AI-powered fraud detection algorithms analyze transaction patterns, behavioral data, and credential issuance trends to identify anomalies that may indicate fraud. While AI-based fraud detection is commonly used in centralized systems, its implementation in decentralized networks requires privacy-preserving techniques such as federated learning and homomorphic encryption. These methods allow AI models to analyze fraud patterns without exposing sensitive user data, maintaining compliance with privacy regulations.

Revocation mechanisms are essential for managing fraud in decentralized identity ecosystems. In centralized systems, identity providers can revoke credentials if fraud is detected. In decentralized systems, revocation must be handled in a way that preserves privacy while ensuring that fraudulent credentials are invalidated. One approach is to use revocation registries, where issuers can publish cryptographic proofs indicating that a credential is no longer valid. This allows verifiers to check the status of a credential without revealing personal details. Zero-knowledge proofs (ZKPs) can further enhance privacy by allowing users to prove that their credentials are still valid without disclosing unnecessary information.

The role of regulatory compliance in decentralized identity fraud prevention cannot be ignored. Many industries, particularly finance and healthcare, require identity verification processes to comply with Know Your Customer (KYC), Anti-Money Laundering (AML), and data protection regulations. While decentralized identity systems offer enhanced privacy, they must also provide mechanisms for lawful oversight and fraud prevention. Governments and regulatory bodies are exploring ways to integrate decentralized identity with existing compliance frameworks while maintaining user control and privacy. One potential solution is the use of privacy-preserving compliance credentials, where users can prove compliance with regulatory requirements without disclosing their full identity.

User education and awareness are also crucial in preventing identity fraud in decentralized ecosystems. Unlike traditional systems, where fraud detection and prevention are managed by service providers, decentralized identity systems place more responsibility on individuals to protect their credentials. Users must be educated on best practices for securing private keys, identifying phishing attempts, and verifying credential authenticity. Identity wallet providers and decentralized identity platforms should implement user-friendly interfaces, security alerts, and step-by-step guidance to help users navigate fraud prevention measures effectively.

Managing identity fraud in a decentralized ecosystem requires a multi-layered approach that combines cryptographic security, identity proofing, reputation-based verification, AI-driven fraud detection, and regulatory compliance. While decentralization reduces the risks associated with centralized data breaches and identity theft, it also shifts fraud prevention responsibilities to a distributed network of participants. By integrating strong authentication mechanisms, privacy-preserving revocation methods, and user education initiatives, decentralized identity systems can enhance security while maintaining the principles of self-sovereign identity and user control.

Compliance and Regulatory Considerations

The adoption of decentralized identity systems presents a significant shift from traditional, centralized identity management models, raising important regulatory and compliance considerations. While self-sovereign identity (SSI) and decentralized identity frameworks aim to enhance privacy, security, and user control, they must also align with legal requirements, industry regulations, and international standards. Governments, financial institutions, healthcare providers, and businesses must navigate a complex regulatory landscape to ensure that decentralized identity solutions comply with existing laws while maintaining their core principles of decentralization and user autonomy.

One of the most critical regulatory considerations for decentralized identity is data protection and privacy compliance. Global data protection laws, such as the General Data Protection Regulation (GDPR) in Europe and the California Consumer Privacy Act (CCPA) in the United States, impose strict rules on how personal data is collected, stored, and processed. These regulations emphasize user consent, data minimization, and the right to access, modify, or delete personal data. Decentralized identity systems align with many of these principles by giving individuals full control over their data and enabling selective disclosure. However, compliance challenges arise when decentralized networks operate across multiple jurisdictions, each with different privacy laws. Ensuring interoperability between decentralized identity solutions and regulatory frameworks requires the development of privacy-preserving mechanisms, such as zero-knowledge proofs (ZKPs) and cryptographic attestations, that allow users to prove identity attributes without exposing unnecessary personal information.

Another key regulatory challenge is Know Your Customer (KYC) and Anti-Money Laundering (AML) compliance. Financial institutions and businesses are required to verify customer identities before providing services to prevent fraud, money laundering, and terrorist financing. Traditional KYC processes involve centralized identity verification, where users submit documents to banks or service providers for validation. Decentralized identity offers a more privacy-preserving approach by allowing users to present verifiable credentials issued by trusted institutions without disclosing excessive personal data. However, regulators must ensure that decentralized identity solutions meet KYC and AML requirements while preserving user privacy. One potential solution is the use of regulatory-compliant verifiable credentials, where users can prove compliance without revealing sensitive information. For example, a user could provide a cryptographic proof of being KYC-verified by a financial institution without sharing underlying documents.

The legal recognition of decentralized identity credentials is another important compliance consideration. Many governments and regulatory bodies require identity documents to be issued by centralized authorities, such as national ID agencies, passport offices, or licensing authorities. While decentralized identity allows for the issuance of verifiable credentials by multiple trusted entities, legal recognition of these credentials varies by jurisdiction. Some countries are exploring blockchain-based identity systems to modernize their digital identity infrastructure, while others remain cautious about recognizing decentralized credentials. Establishing legal frameworks that accept decentralized identity as a valid form of identification is essential for widespread adoption. Governments must work closely with identity providers, industry stakeholders, and international organizations to create policies that support decentralized identity while ensuring trust and security.

Cross-border identity verification is another regulatory challenge in decentralized identity. In a globalized economy, individuals frequently need to verify their identity across different countries for purposes such as travel, employment, banking, and e-commerce. Traditional identity systems rely on government-issued passports, visas, and national ID cards, which must be verified manually by institutions. Decentralized identity offers a way to streamline cross-border verification by enabling users to carry portable, verifiable credentials that can be authenticated anywhere. However, achieving regulatory acceptance for cross-border decentralized identity solutions requires harmonization between different legal systems. Initiatives such as the European Blockchain Services Infrastructure (EBSI) are working to create interoperable digital identity frameworks that allow credentials to be recognized across multiple countries.

Regulatory compliance also extends to consumer protection and fraud prevention. Decentralized identity empowers users by giving them control over their personal data, but it also introduces new risks, such as identity fraud and credential forgery. Regulators must ensure that decentralized identity systems include mechanisms for credential revocation, fraud detection, and dispute resolution. Unlike centralized systems, where identity fraud can be reported to a central authority, decentralized networks require decentralized governance models to handle fraudulent activities. Implementing decentralized reputation systems, identity trust frameworks, and fraud-resistant verification protocols can help address these concerns while maintaining compliance with consumer protection laws.

Intellectual property and data ownership regulations are also relevant to decentralized identity. In traditional digital identity systems, service providers retain control over user data, often monetizing it through targeted advertising or analytics. Decentralized identity shifts data ownership to individuals, raising legal questions about how personal data is controlled, transferred, and protected under different regulatory frameworks. Governments must establish clear guidelines on data ownership rights, ensuring that users have legal authority over their digital identities while preventing misuse by third parties.

Regulatory frameworks must also address the role of decentralized autonomous organizations (DAOs) and decentralized identity governance models. As decentralized identity ecosystems evolve, governance decisions are increasingly being made through decentralized networks rather than centralized institutions. Regulators must determine how to oversee DAOs and decentralized identity providers while maintaining compliance with national and international laws. Establishing legal definitions for decentralized entities, creating mechanisms for dispute resolution, and ensuring accountability within decentralized networks are essential steps in integrating decentralized identity into regulatory frameworks.

The balance between compliance and innovation is a central challenge for regulators and industry stakeholders. Overly restrictive regulations could hinder the adoption of decentralized identity by imposing unnecessary barriers, while a lack of regulatory oversight could lead to security vulnerabilities and misuse. A collaborative approach between governments, technology providers, financial institutions, and privacy advocates is necessary to create policies that enable decentralized identity to thrive while maintaining legal and ethical safeguards. Regulatory sandboxes, where decentralized identity solutions can be tested in controlled environments before full deployment, provide a valuable way to explore compliance challenges while fostering innovation.

The evolving nature of digital identity regulations requires ongoing dialogue between policymakers, industry leaders, and user communities. As decentralized identity systems continue to develop, regulatory frameworks must be adaptable to new technologies, emerging threats, and changing user needs. Creating interoperable, privacy-preserving, and legally recognized decentralized identity solutions will require governments to embrace forward-thinking policies that prioritize security, transparency, and individual rights. By addressing compliance and regulatory considerations proactively, decentralized identity can achieve mainstream acceptance while ensuring a secure, fair, and legally compliant digital identity ecosystem.

AI and Decentralized Identity: Opportunities and Risks

The convergence of artificial intelligence (AI) and decentralized identity is shaping the future of digital identity management, offering both promising opportunities and potential risks. AI has transformed the way identity verification, fraud detection, and access management are conducted, while decentralized identity provides a new framework that enhances user privacy, security, and control. By integrating AI into decentralized identity ecosystems, organizations can streamline authentication processes, detect fraudulent activities more effectively, and improve user experience. However, this fusion also introduces ethical, security, and privacy concerns that must be carefully addressed to prevent unintended consequences.

One of the most significant opportunities AI brings to decentralized identity is automation in identity verification and authentication. Traditional identity verification methods rely on manual processes, such as document checks, in-person verification, and centralized databases. AI-powered solutions, particularly those using machine learning and computer vision, can automate identity verification by analyzing biometric data, detecting forged documents, and assessing behavioral patterns. When combined with decentralized identity frameworks, AI-driven verification allows users to prove their identity in real time without relying on centralized intermediaries. This reduces onboarding times for financial services, e-government platforms, and digital applications while ensuring secure, fraud-resistant verification.

Fraud detection is another area where AI enhances decentralized identity. Identity fraud, including synthetic identity fraud, credential theft, and account takeovers, poses a significant risk in both centralized and decentralized identity ecosystems. AI-driven fraud detection models analyze large datasets to identify patterns associated with fraudulent behavior, such as inconsistencies in credential usage, abnormal authentication attempts, and suspicious transaction histories. In decentralized identity systems, AI can be used to detect anomalies in identity credentials without compromising user privacy. Federated learning, a privacy-preserving AI technique, allows AI models to train on decentralized datasets without exposing personal information, enabling fraud detection without centralizing identity data.

AI also improves user experience in decentralized identity applications. Many decentralized identity solutions require users to manage cryptographic keys, verifiable credentials, and identity wallets, which can be complex for non-technical individuals. AI-powered identity assistants can simplify these processes by guiding users through key management, authentication, and identity recovery. Natural language processing (NLP) allows AI assistants to interact with users conversationally, providing step-by-step support in managing their digital identity. Additionally, AI can analyze user behavior to offer personalized security recommendations, such as suggesting stronger authentication methods or detecting potential security risks.

The integration of AI with decentralized identity also presents opportunities for dynamic access control and identity management. Traditional access control mechanisms use static rules, such as passwords and predefined role-based permissions. AI-driven adaptive authentication adjusts access levels based on real-time risk assessments, analyzing factors such as device security, geolocation, and login behavior. If an AI system detects unusual login attempts or signs of identity compromise, it can trigger additional authentication steps, such as biometric verification or multi-factor authentication (MFA). This enhances security while maintaining user convenience.

Despite these advantages, AI in decentralized identity systems comes with several risks and challenges. One of the primary concerns is privacy. AI models require large datasets to improve accuracy and efficiency, but collecting and processing identity data raises significant privacy concerns. Decentralized identity systems are designed to minimize data exposure, allowing users to retain control over their personal information. However, AI-driven identity verification processes may inadvertently collect and analyze more data than necessary, potentially violating privacy regulations. Ensuring that AI models adhere to privacy-enhancing techniques, such as differential privacy and zero-knowledge proofs (ZKPs), is essential to preventing data misuse.

Bias in AI algorithms is another major risk in decentralized identity systems. AI models trained on biased datasets can reinforce discrimination in identity verification and access control. For example, facial recognition systems have been shown to exhibit racial, gender, and age biases, leading to inaccuracies in biometric authentication. In decentralized identity, biased AI models could result in certain groups experiencing higher rates of authentication failures or access denials. Addressing AI bias requires careful dataset curation, transparency in algorithmic decision-making, and ongoing monitoring to detect and mitigate discriminatory patterns.

Security vulnerabilities in AI models also pose a risk to decentralized identity. AI systems are susceptible to adversarial attacks, where malicious actors manipulate AI models to produce incorrect outputs. In the context of identity verification, adversarial attacks could involve altering biometric data or injecting manipulated credentials into an AI model to bypass authentication checks. Ensuring the robustness of AI-driven identity verification systems requires continuous testing, adversarial training, and the implementation of multi-layered security mechanisms to detect and prevent AI model manipulation.

The role of AI in identity governance and trust mechanisms also raises ethical concerns. Decentralized identity systems operate without centralized authorities, relying on trust frameworks to verify credentials and identity claims. AI-driven trust scoring, which assigns reputation scores based on user behavior and credential history, could introduce algorithmic bias and reduce transparency in decision-making. Users may face challenges in understanding how AI systems assess their credibility, leading to potential discrimination or exclusion from services. Implementing explainable AI (XAI) techniques, which provide transparent insights into AI decision-making processes, can help address this challenge and ensure fairness in decentralized identity ecosystems.

Another significant challenge is the regulatory landscape surrounding AI and decentralized identity. Many governments are developing AI regulations to address issues related to algorithmic fairness, data protection, and accountability. At the same time, decentralized identity frameworks must comply with existing identity regulations, such as Know Your Customer (KYC) requirements, Anti-Money Laundering (AML) laws, and data privacy mandates. The intersection of AI and decentralized identity requires careful regulatory alignment to ensure compliance while preserving innovation. Regulatory sandboxes, where AI-driven identity solutions can be tested under controlled conditions, provide an opportunity for policymakers and industry stakeholders to explore compliance strategies.

Interoperability between AI-driven identity verification systems and decentralized identity standards is another area of concern. Various identity providers, blockchain networks, and AI-powered authentication platforms operate with different technical architectures, making seamless integration challenging. Standardizing AI protocols for identity verification, credential issuance, and fraud detection is essential for ensuring interoperability across different identity ecosystems. Organizations such as the Decentralized Identity Foundation (DIF) and the World Wide Web Consortium (W3C) are working on identity interoperability frameworks that incorporate AI-driven authentication while maintaining decentralized principles.

As AI and decentralized identity continue to evolve, striking a balance between innovation, security, privacy, and compliance is essential. AI has the potential to enhance decentralized identity by improving verification accuracy, reducing fraud, and enabling adaptive authentication. However, the risks associated with privacy violations, bias, adversarial attacks, and regulatory uncertainty must be addressed through careful design, transparent governance, and privacy-enhancing AI techniques. By ensuring ethical AI development, robust security measures, and compliance with legal frameworks, AI and decentralized identity can work together to create a more secure, efficient, and user-centric digital identity ecosystem.

Quantum Computing and Identity Security

Quantum computing is poised to revolutionize many aspects of technology, including cryptography, cybersecurity, and identity management. While classical computers rely on binary processing (bits representing 0s and 1s), quantum computers leverage quantum bits (qubits) that can exist in multiple states simultaneously due to the principles of superposition and entanglement. This capability allows quantum computers to perform complex calculations at exponentially higher speeds than traditional systems, presenting both opportunities and significant risks for digital identity security.

One of the most critical concerns regarding quantum computing is its potential to break existing cryptographic systems. Modern digital identity systems rely heavily on asymmetric cryptography, particularly public-key infrastructure (PKI) algorithms such as RSA, Elliptic Curve Cryptography (ECC), and Diffie-Hellman key exchange. These encryption methods depend on the mathematical difficulty of factoring large prime numbers or solving discrete logarithm problems—tasks that are practically infeasible for classical computers but could be efficiently solved by a sufficiently powerful quantum computer. If quantum computing reaches an advanced stage, widely used cryptographic methods securing digital identities, blockchain networks, and authentication systems could become obsolete.

Shor's algorithm, a quantum algorithm developed by mathematician Peter Shor, demonstrates how quantum computers can efficiently factor large numbers, posing a direct threat to RSA encryption. If a sufficiently large quantum computer is built, it could decrypt encrypted communications, impersonate users, forge digital signatures, and break blockchain-based decentralized identity frameworks. The implications of this breakthrough would be severe, as sensitive identity data, financial transactions, and governmental records currently protected by conventional cryptographic methods would be vulnerable to quantum attacks.

To mitigate these risks, researchers and cryptographers are actively developing quantum-resistant cryptographic algorithms, often referred to as post-quantum cryptography (PQC). These algorithms are designed to withstand attacks from both classical and quantum computers, ensuring that digital identities remain secure even in a post-quantum era. The National Institute of Standards and Technology (NIST) has been leading global efforts to standardize post-quantum cryptographic algorithms, evaluating new approaches such as lattice-based cryptography, hash-based cryptography, multivariate polynomial cryptography, and code-based cryptography. Governments, businesses, and identity providers must begin transitioning to these quantum-resistant techniques to safeguard digital identities from future threats.

Blockchain-based decentralized identity solutions, which depend on cryptographic hash functions and digital signatures, are also at risk from quantum attacks. While hash functions such as SHA-256 are currently considered quantum-resistant to some extent, the digital signatures used in blockchain transactions and identity attestations could be broken by quantum computers. This vulnerability raises concerns about the integrity and security of self-sovereign identity (SSI) systems, which rely on blockchain for tamper-proof identity verification. To address this challenge, blockchain networks must explore quantum-resistant digital signature schemes, such as lattice-based signatures and hash-based signatures, to maintain security in a quantum future.

Another area where quantum computing could impact identity security is in authentication mechanisms. Current authentication systems rely on password-based login methods, biometric verification, and multi-factor authentication (MFA). While quantum computers may not directly impact password security (since brute-force attacks would still be constrained by entropy limitations), they could enhance AI-driven attacks capable of predicting user behaviors, generating sophisticated phishing attacks, or breaking biometric templates. Ensuring that authentication systems adopt quantum-resistant encryption and AI-driven anomaly detection will be crucial to maintaining security.

Quantum key distribution (QKD) is one promising application of quantum computing that could enhance identity security rather than threaten it. QKD uses quantum mechanics to create encryption keys that are theoretically immune to interception or decryption. Because any attempt to measure a quantum state disturbs it, QKD enables the secure exchange of cryptographic keys, ensuring end-to-end encrypted communication between users and identity verification systems. Governments and technology companies are actively researching QKD as a method for securing sensitive identity transactions and communications in the post-quantum era.

The transition to quantum-resistant identity security presents logistical and technical challenges. Many existing digital identity systems, including government-issued eIDs, banking authentication protocols, and enterprise access management platforms, are deeply integrated with classical cryptographic methods. Upgrading these systems to support post-quantum cryptography requires extensive testing, infrastructure modifications, and standardization efforts. Organizations must begin implementing hybrid cryptographic approaches, combining classical and quantum-resistant encryption, to ensure a seamless transition while quantum technology continues to evolve.

Regulatory and compliance considerations also play a role in quantum-resistant identity security. Governments and regulatory bodies must establish policies that mandate the adoption of quantum-safe cryptographic standards, ensuring that identity providers, financial institutions, and digital service platforms remain secure against future quantum threats. Cybersecurity frameworks such as GDPR, HIPAA, and PCI-DSS must evolve to address the risks posed by quantum computing, requiring organizations to demonstrate compliance with post-quantum security measures.

User education and awareness are critical in preparing for the post-quantum era. Many individuals and businesses are unaware of the risks that quantum computing poses to digital identity security. Public awareness campaigns, cybersecurity training programs, and industry collaborations are essential to ensuring that users understand the importance of transitioning to quantum-resistant identity solutions. Organizations must also develop user-friendly identity management interfaces that support quantum-safe authentication without compromising convenience or accessibility.

The role of AI in quantum computing further complicates the landscape of identity security. AI-driven quantum algorithms could enhance identity verification processes by enabling more accurate biometric authentication, fraud detection, and behavioral analysis. However, if malicious actors gain access to quantum-powered AI, they could exploit vulnerabilities in identity systems at an unprecedented scale. Ensuring that quantum AI is used ethically and securely in identity verification will require strict governance frameworks, transparency in algorithmic decision-making, and ongoing security research.

Despite the challenges, quantum computing also presents opportunities for strengthening identity security. Quantum encryption methods, secure multi-party computation, and quantum-safe authentication protocols offer new ways to protect user identities in digital ecosystems. Governments, enterprises, and research institutions must collaborate to develop and implement quantum-resistant identity frameworks, ensuring that individuals retain control over their digital identities while remaining protected from emerging cyber threats.

As quantum computing continues to advance, identity security must evolve in parallel. Organizations must proactively assess their cryptographic infrastructure, invest in quantum-resistant security measures, and stay informed about the latest developments in post-quantum cryptography. By preparing for the quantum future today, businesses and individuals can ensure that their digital identities remain secure, resilient, and trustworthy in an era of unprecedented computational power.

Identity and the Metaverse: A New Digital World

The emergence of the metaverse represents a fundamental shift in how people interact, socialize, and conduct business in digital environments. As virtual worlds become more immersive and interconnected, digital identity takes on an even greater significance. Identity in the metaverse is not just about authentication and access control but also about self-expression, reputation, and trust in decentralized virtual spaces. Managing identity in this new digital world requires innovative solutions that balance security, privacy, and user sovereignty while ensuring seamless interoperability across different platforms and virtual experiences.

In traditional online ecosystems, digital identity is often fragmented, tied to centralized platforms such as social media accounts, gaming profiles, and corporate logins. Each of these platforms manages user credentials separately, requiring individuals to create and maintain multiple accounts across different services. This results in an inefficient and disjointed identity experience, where users must repeatedly verify their identities and personal information. In contrast, the metaverse envisions a seamless, persistent identity that allows individuals to navigate multiple virtual spaces while maintaining control over their personal data and digital assets.

Self-sovereign identity (SSI) and decentralized identity frameworks provide a promising foundation for identity in the metaverse. Instead of relying on centralized entities to issue and manage digital identities, SSI enables individuals to create, control, and verify their own identities using cryptographic credentials. These verifiable credentials can be stored in digital wallets and selectively shared with different metaverse platforms, allowing users to prove their identity without revealing excessive personal information. This approach enhances privacy, reduces the risk of identity theft, and eliminates the need for platform-specific logins.

One of the key challenges in metaverse identity management is establishing trust in virtual interactions. Unlike the physical world, where identity is often tied to government-issued documents or in-person verification, the metaverse requires new methods for proving identity and reputation in fully digital environments. Verifiable credentials allow users to authenticate their real-world identity while preserving anonymity when needed. For example, an individual might use a verifiable credential to prove they are of legal age to access restricted content without revealing their full name or date of birth.

Similarly, professional credentials can be used to verify expertise in virtual workplaces without exposing unnecessary personal details.

Digital ownership and asset management are also closely tied to identity in the metaverse. Users acquire virtual goods, property, and digital collectibles in metaverse environments, often represented as non-fungible tokens (NFTs) or blockchain-based assets. Ensuring that these assets are securely linked to a user's identity is crucial for preventing fraud, theft, and unauthorized access. Decentralized identity solutions enable users to establish provable ownership of digital assets, allowing for secure transfers, cross-platform compatibility, and persistent asset management.

Interoperability is another critical factor in metaverse identity. The metaverse is not a single, unified platform but rather a collection of interconnected virtual worlds, games, and digital experiences developed by different organizations and communities. Users should be able to carry their identity, reputation, and digital assets across these environments without being locked into a single provider. Open identity standards, such as those developed by the World Wide Web Consortium (W3C) and the Decentralized Identity Foundation (DIF), can facilitate interoperability, ensuring that users maintain control over their identity regardless of the platform they choose to engage with.

Privacy concerns in the metaverse are also more complex than in traditional digital spaces. Virtual environments collect vast amounts of personal data, including biometric information, behavioral analytics, and interaction histories. Unlike web-based services, where users interact through text and static profiles, the metaverse introduces real-time avatars, voice interactions, and motion tracking, increasing the scope of identity-related data that can be collected. Without robust privacy protections, this data could be exploited for surveillance, targeted advertising, or identity manipulation. Privacy-preserving technologies, such as zero-knowledge proofs (ZKPs) and decentralized identity wallets, allow users to verify their credentials without exposing sensitive information, ensuring greater control over personal data in the metaverse.

Security threats such as identity theft, deepfake impersonation, and avatar fraud pose significant risks to metaverse identity management. Deepfake technology can be used to manipulate voice and facial features, creating convincing digital impersonations that undermine trust in virtual spaces. Similarly, identity theft in the metaverse could involve hijacking avatars, stealing digital assets, or assuming false credentials. Decentralized identity solutions, combined with AI-driven fraud detection and biometric authentication, can help mitigate these risks by ensuring that users maintain secure and verifiable control over their metaverse identities.

The economic implications of identity in the metaverse extend beyond individual users to businesses, brands, and virtual economies. Companies establishing a presence in the metaverse must verify their brand identity, ensuring that customers and users can distinguish official entities from imposters. Fraudulent actors could exploit decentralized environments to create fake brand representations, misleading consumers and damaging reputations. Verifiable credentials for corporate identities, domain-linked identity verification, and decentralized trust registries can help businesses establish authenticity and protect their brand presence in virtual worlds.

Regulatory and legal frameworks for identity in the metaverse are still in their early stages. Governments and policymakers are beginning to explore how existing digital identity regulations, such as Know Your Customer (KYC) and data protection laws, apply to fully virtual environments. Ensuring compliance with international legal standards while preserving the decentralized nature of metaverse identity is a challenge that will require collaboration between regulators, technology developers, and privacy advocates. Legal recognition of decentralized identity credentials, cross-border identity verification mechanisms, and ethical guidelines for avatar representation are among the key areas that need to be addressed.

As metaverse adoption grows, the social and ethical aspects of digital identity will become increasingly important. Identity in virtual worlds is not limited to real-world credentials but also includes self-expression through avatars, pseudonymous identities, and virtual personas. Users may choose to represent themselves differently in various metaverse contexts, from professional environments to gaming and entertainment. Ensuring that metaverse identity systems respect diversity, inclusivity, and user autonomy while preventing discrimination, harassment, and identity exploitation is a complex but necessary consideration.

The future of identity in the metaverse will be shaped by technological advancements, governance frameworks, and evolving user expectations. Decentralized identity provides a foundation for secure, user-controlled identity management, enabling individuals to navigate the metaverse with greater privacy, security, and trust. As virtual worlds become more integrated into daily life, the development of ethical, interoperable, and privacy-preserving identity solutions will be essential for building a metaverse that empowers users while maintaining the integrity of digital interactions.

SSI and the Internet of Things (IoT)

The rapid expansion of the Internet of Things (IoT) has transformed how devices interact with each other and with users. From smart homes and connected cars to industrial automation and healthcare monitoring, IoT devices generate and exchange vast amounts of data. However, managing identity and access control in IoT environments presents significant challenges. Traditional identity models, which rely on centralized authorities, struggle to provide scalable, secure, and efficient authentication for billions of interconnected devices. Self-sovereign identity (SSI) offers a decentralized approach to IoT identity management, enabling secure, user-controlled authentication and access control while reducing reliance on centralized systems.

One of the core challenges in IoT security is device authentication. Traditional authentication methods, such as username-password combinations and API keys, are not suitable for IoT devices due to their limited processing power and the need for automated, seamless communication. SSI provides a decentralized alternative by allowing IoT devices to have unique, verifiable identities using decentralized identifiers (DIDs) and verifiable credentials (VCs). Instead of relying on a central authority to validate device identity, SSI enables each device to authenticate itself cryptographically, ensuring that only trusted devices can communicate within a network.

Decentralized identity in IoT enhances security by eliminating the need for a single point of failure. Centralized identity management systems, such as cloud-based authentication services, are vulnerable to cyberattacks, data breaches, and system failures. If a centralized IoT identity provider is compromised, attackers can gain unauthorized access to connected devices, leading to potential security risks such as hijacking smart home systems, disrupting industrial operations, or tampering with medical devices. By leveraging SSI, IoT ecosystems can distribute trust across multiple entities, ensuring that identity verification is more resilient to attacks.

Interoperability is another significant challenge in IoT identity management. Different manufacturers and service providers use proprietary authentication mechanisms, creating fragmented ecosystems where devices struggle to communicate securely across platforms. SSI introduces a standardized approach to IoT identity, allowing devices from different vendors to authenticate and interact without relying on closed, centralized systems. Through open identity standards such as those developed by the World Wide Web Consortium (W3C) and the Decentralized Identity Foundation (DIF), SSI enables cross-platform compatibility, ensuring that IoT devices can securely interact regardless of their manufacturer or service provider.

IoT devices often collect and transmit sensitive personal data, raising privacy concerns. Smart home devices, wearable health monitors, and connected vehicles generate detailed user behavior patterns, which can be exploited for surveillance, targeted advertising, or malicious attacks if not properly secured. Traditional identity models require users to trust centralized entities with their data, often without full transparency on how it is stored or shared. SSI empowers users by giving them control over their IoT-related identity and data sharing preferences. Using privacy-preserving techniques such as zero-knowledge proofs (ZKPs), users can grant IoT devices permission to access specific data without revealing unnecessary personal information.

In industrial IoT (IIoT) environments, where connected sensors and automation systems play a crucial role in manufacturing, supply chain logistics, and energy management, SSI enhances security and efficiency. Industrial systems require reliable machine-to-machine

(M2M) authentication to prevent unauthorized access and cyber threats. SSI enables industrial IoT devices to establish trust autonomously, reducing reliance on centralized identity providers. By using verifiable credentials, IIoT systems can ensure that only authorized machines, operators, and applications access critical infrastructure, preventing industrial espionage, sabotage, and data breaches.

Smart cities also benefit from the integration of SSI with IoT. Urban infrastructure increasingly relies on IoT devices for traffic management, energy distribution, waste management, and public safety. Managing digital identity across a vast network of connected sensors, vehicles, and infrastructure components requires a scalable and secure solution. SSI allows municipal authorities to issue verifiable credentials to smart city IoT devices, ensuring that only trusted entities can access and control urban services. This approach reduces the risk of cyberattacks on public infrastructure while enabling seamless citizen interactions with smart city services.

The combination of SSI and IoT also improves supply chain transparency and product authentication. IoT-enabled supply chains use connected sensors and tracking devices to monitor the movement of goods, ensuring that products remain secure and comply with regulations. However, verifying the identity of these tracking devices and ensuring that supply chain data is tamper-proof is a challenge. SSI enables manufacturers, suppliers, and logistics providers to issue verifiable credentials to IoT devices, allowing stakeholders to authenticate product origins, track shipments, and verify compliance with industry standards. This reduces the risk of counterfeit goods, unauthorized alterations, and supply chain fraud.

Security threats such as botnets and distributed denial-of-service (DDoS) attacks are major concerns in IoT networks. Many IoT devices are vulnerable to being compromised and used in large-scale cyberattacks, as seen in incidents where unsecured connected cameras and routers were exploited to launch massive DDoS attacks. SSI mitigates these threats by requiring strong, cryptographically verifiable identity authentication for IoT devices. By eliminating weak, default credentials and enforcing decentralized authentication, SSI reduces the likelihood of IoT devices being hijacked for malicious activities.

Despite its benefits, implementing SSI in IoT presents several challenges. One of the primary obstacles is the limited processing power of many IoT devices, which may not be capable of handling complex cryptographic operations. To address this, lightweight cryptographic techniques and hardware-based security modules can be used to enable SSI authentication on resource-constrained devices. Additionally, edge computing can be leveraged to offload identity verification tasks to nearby computing nodes, reducing the processing burden on IoT devices while maintaining decentralized security.

Regulatory and legal considerations also play a role in the adoption of SSI for IoT. Many industries, particularly healthcare, finance, and critical infrastructure, must comply with stringent security and data protection regulations. Governments and regulatory bodies must establish guidelines that define how decentralized identity frameworks can be integrated into IoT security compliance requirements. Ensuring that SSI-based IoT identity solutions align with existing data protection laws, such as the General Data Protection Regulation (GDPR) and industry-specific security standards, is crucial for widespread adoption.

As IoT networks continue to expand, integrating SSI provides a pathway toward more secure, privacy-preserving, and interoperable identity management. By eliminating centralized vulnerabilities, enabling user control over data sharing, and facilitating trusted device interactions, SSI strengthens the foundation for a more secure and scalable IoT ecosystem. The continued development of decentralized identity standards, lightweight cryptographic protocols, and regulatory frameworks will be essential in realizing the full potential of SSI in IoT environments.

The Role of Decentralized Autonomous Organizations (DAOs)

Decentralized Autonomous Organizations (DAOs) are reshaping governance, decision-making, and coordination in digital ecosystems. Built on blockchain technology, DAOs enable decentralized governance structures where participants collectively make decisions without relying on traditional hierarchical management. These organizations operate using smart contracts, ensuring that rules are enforced transparently and autonomously. As DAOs grow in adoption across industries, their role in identity management, self-sovereign identity (SSI), and decentralized trust networks becomes increasingly important.

One of the most significant contributions of DAOs to identity management is their ability to act as decentralized trust anchors. Traditional identity verification models depend on centralized institutions such as governments, banks, and corporations to issue and validate credentials. This reliance creates vulnerabilities, including data breaches, censorship risks, and exclusionary barriers. DAOs introduce a decentralized approach to trust, where identity verification is governed by a distributed network of participants rather than a single authority. Through decentralized governance, DAOs can issue, validate, and revoke verifiable credentials in a transparent and censorship-resistant manner.

DAOs also play a crucial role in governing self-sovereign identity ecosystems. SSI empowers individuals to control their digital identities, but ensuring trust in identity credentials requires robust governance mechanisms. DAOs can facilitate decentralized identity governance by establishing community-driven policies for credential issuance, revocation, and dispute resolution. Instead of relying on a central entity to oversee identity standards, DAOs allow participants to vote on policies, ensuring that identity systems remain fair, inclusive, and adaptable to evolving needs.

One application of DAOs in identity management is reputation-based identity verification. Traditional identity systems often rely on government-issued documents to establish trust, but in decentralized environments, reputation and community attestations can serve as an alternative. DAOs can implement decentralized reputation systems where individuals earn trust over time through verifiable interactions, endorsements, and contributions to the network. For example, in a DAO-managed freelance marketplace, workers could accumulate reputation credentials based on completed projects, client reviews, and peer validation. These credentials, stored in a decentralized identity wallet, would allow users to prove their expertise and reliability across multiple platforms.

DAOs also enhance privacy and security in identity systems. Centralized identity providers collect and store vast amounts of personal data, making them attractive targets for cyberattacks. A breach in a centralized system can expose millions of users' sensitive information. In contrast, DAOs distribute identity verification across multiple nodes, reducing the risk of a single point of failure. Additionally, DAOs can integrate privacy-preserving technologies such as zero-knowledge proofs (ZKPs), enabling users to verify credentials without exposing personal details. This approach strengthens privacy protections while maintaining trust in identity claims.

The governance of digital identity standards is another area where DAOs play a pivotal role. Decentralized identity frameworks require global standards to ensure interoperability across platforms, industries, and jurisdictions. Traditionally, these standards are developed by centralized organizations or regulatory bodies, which may not fully represent the interests of decentralized communities. DAOs offer an alternative governance model where stakeholders— including developers, identity providers, and end-users—participate in the decision-making process for identity standards. By leveraging token-based voting and smart contract enforcement, DAOs create transparent, democratic governance structures for digital identity protocols.

The integration of DAOs with decentralized finance (DeFi) is another area where identity and governance intersect. Many DeFi platforms require identity verification for regulatory compliance, loan issuance, and fraud prevention. DAOs can establish decentralized KYC (Know Your Customer) frameworks, where users submit verifiable credentials without revealing excessive personal information. By using self-sovereign identity solutions, DAOs enable DeFi platforms to comply with financial regulations while preserving user privacy and autonomy. This approach aligns with the principles of decentralization, reducing reliance on centralized KYC providers while ensuring that DeFi ecosystems remain secure and compliant.

DAOs also provide new models for organizational identity. Traditional businesses rely on corporate registries, legal entities, and government oversight to establish their legitimacy. In decentralized ecosystems, DAOs can issue and manage organizational identities through verifiable credentials, allowing businesses to operate transparently and autonomously on blockchain networks. A DAO-governed business could use decentralized identity to verify its legitimacy, establish trust with partners and customers, and streamline regulatory compliance through cryptographic proofs. This model reduces bureaucratic inefficiencies and enables more agile, decentralized business structures.

Another key function of DAOs in identity management is dispute resolution. Traditional identity systems rely on legal frameworks and centralized institutions to handle identity disputes, such as fraudulent claims, identity theft, or credential revocation. DAOs introduce decentralized dispute resolution mechanisms, where community members collectively review and resolve identity-related conflicts. By leveraging decentralized courts, arbitration protocols, and smart contract-based enforcement, DAOs create transparent and fair dispute resolution systems that do not depend on centralized authorities.

The role of DAOs extends beyond identity governance to broader social and political applications. Digital citizenship, decentralized voting, and community-driven governance models all benefit from the decentralized coordination enabled by DAOs. For example, a decentralized city governance DAO could issue verifiable credentials to residents, allowing them to vote on local policies, access public services, and participate in civic engagement. This model reduces bureaucracy, enhances transparency, and empowers citizens with greater control over their digital and physical identities.

Despite their potential, DAOs face challenges in identity governance. Legal recognition of DAOs remains an evolving issue, with many jurisdictions lacking clear regulations on their status as legal entities. Without formal legal recognition, DAOs may face obstacles in enforcing agreements, managing disputes, and interacting with traditional institutions. Additionally, DAO governance mechanisms, such as token-based voting, must address issues of voter participation, governance centralization, and security risks such as Sybil attacks. Ensuring that DAO governance models remain fair, decentralized, and resistant to manipulation is critical for their long-term success in identity management.

Scalability is another challenge for DAOs in identity governance. As decentralized identity ecosystems grow, the number of governance decisions, credential issuances, and dispute resolutions managed by DAOs will increase. Ensuring that DAOs can handle high transaction volumes efficiently without compromising decentralization requires innovations in blockchain scalability, layer-2 solutions, and decentralized governance protocols. Developing automated, trust-minimized identity verification processes that reduce governance overhead while maintaining transparency will be essential for scaling DAO-based identity frameworks.

The evolution of DAOs in digital identity represents a shift towards more transparent, user-controlled, and community-driven governance models. By enabling decentralized trust frameworks, reputation-based verification, and fair dispute resolution, DAOs play a crucial role in shaping the future of self-sovereign identity. As technology, regulation, and adoption continue to evolve, DAOs will serve as a foundational element of decentralized identity systems, ensuring that digital identity remains secure, interoperable, and aligned with the principles of decentralization.

Designing User-Friendly Identity Wallets

As digital identity systems evolve, identity wallets have emerged as a critical component of decentralized identity management. These wallets allow users to store, manage, and present verifiable credentials securely while maintaining control over their personal data. However, for decentralized identity solutions to achieve widespread adoption, identity wallets must be designed with usability in mind. A user-friendly identity wallet should provide security, accessibility, and seamless integration while minimizing complexity for non-technical users. Designing an effective identity wallet requires balancing security with ease of use, ensuring that individuals can navigate their digital identities without friction.

One of the primary challenges in designing identity wallets is private key management. Unlike traditional identity systems where a central authority manages user authentication, decentralized identity wallets place the responsibility of securing cryptographic keys directly on users. If a private key is lost or stolen, access to credentials and digital identities can be permanently compromised. To address this, identity wallets should incorporate user-friendly recovery mechanisms such as social recovery, multi-signature authentication, or biometric-based access controls. These features provide users with alternative ways to regain access to their wallets without relying on centralized recovery services, preserving the principles of self-sovereign identity (SSI).

The user interface (UI) and user experience (UX) of an identity wallet play a crucial role in adoption. Many decentralized applications suffer from poor UX, which can discourage users from engaging with the technology. Identity wallets should have intuitive navigation, clear prompts, and simplified workflows that guide users through key actions such as credential issuance, verification, and sharing. Visual indicators, such as trust levels or credential expiration alerts, help users understand the status of their digital identities at a glance. Ensuring that identity wallets are accessible to users with different levels of technical expertise will be key to their success.

Interoperability is another essential factor in designing user-friendly identity wallets. A well-designed wallet should support multiple identity standards, such as decentralized identifiers (DIDs) and verifiable credentials (VCs), to ensure compatibility across various identity providers, blockchain networks, and authentication platforms. Users should be able to store credentials from different issuers—such as governments, educational institutions, and financial services— without being locked into a single ecosystem. Adhering to open standards, such as those developed by the World Wide Web Consortium (W3C) and the Decentralized Identity Foundation (DIF), ensures that identity wallets remain flexible and future-proof.

Security remains a fundamental concern when designing identity wallets. While decentralized identity reduces reliance on centralized databases, it also introduces new risks, such as phishing attacks, credential theft, and unauthorized access. Identity wallets must implement robust security measures, including end-to-end encryption, hardware-based security modules, and secure enclaves for storing cryptographic keys. Multi-factor authentication (MFA) should be integrated into wallet access, ensuring that even if a device is compromised, attackers cannot easily gain control of user credentials. Additionally, wallets should provide real-time alerts and notifications for suspicious activities, enabling users to respond proactively to potential security threats.

Privacy-enhancing features are also critical for identity wallets. Unlike traditional identity verification systems that often require users to disclose excessive personal information, decentralized identity wallets should enable selective disclosure. Users should be able to share only the minimum amount of information necessary for verification using zero-knowledge proofs (ZKPs) and other cryptographic techniques. For example, instead of revealing a full government ID to prove age eligibility, a wallet should allow users to share a cryptographic proof confirming they are over a certain age without exposing additional details. This approach enhances privacy and reduces data exposure risks.

Another aspect of user-friendly identity wallet design is seamless credential management. Users should be able to organize and categorize credentials efficiently, ensuring they can quickly locate and present the right credential when needed. Features such as credential grouping, search functionality, and automatic expiration reminders help users manage their digital identities effectively. Wallets should also support offline verification, allowing users to present credentials in environments with limited internet access while maintaining security and authenticity.

Mobile accessibility is essential for identity wallets, as most users rely on smartphones for digital interactions. A mobile-first design ensures that identity wallets are available on the go, enabling users to verify credentials, access services, and authenticate transactions from their devices. However, mobile platforms also introduce security risks, such as malware and unauthorized access. Ensuring that identity wallets integrate with secure mobile environments, leverage biometric authentication (such as fingerprint or facial recognition), and offer remote wipe capabilities in case of device theft enhances security while maintaining usability.

The integration of identity wallets with existing authentication systems is another factor in driving adoption. Users should be able to use their identity wallets for passwordless authentication, replacing traditional login credentials with decentralized authentication methods. Identity wallets can generate cryptographic signatures that verify user identity without requiring passwords, reducing the risk of credential leaks and phishing attacks. This approach simplifies authentication for users while improving overall security.

User education and onboarding are crucial components of identity wallet adoption. Since decentralized identity is a relatively new concept for many users, wallets should include built-in tutorials, guided setup processes, and contextual explanations to help users understand key concepts such as verifiable credentials, private key security, and identity verification. Providing clear and simple explanations of how identity wallets work increases user confidence and reduces the risk of errors.

Cross-platform functionality enhances the usability of identity wallets by allowing users to access their credentials across different devices and operating systems. Users should be able to sync their identity wallets securely between their smartphones, tablets, and desktops while maintaining privacy and security. Cloud backup solutions with end-to-end encryption can enable secure cross-device synchronization while ensuring that private keys remain protected from unauthorized access.

Identity wallets also need to support secure sharing mechanisms. In many cases, users need to share credentials with verifiers, such as employers, government agencies, or online service providers. Implementing secure QR code-based sharing, encrypted data transmission, and decentralized verification protocols ensures that credentials are shared securely without the risk of interception or tampering. Additionally, integrating consent management features allows users to track and revoke access to shared credentials, maintaining control over their digital identity at all times.

The adoption of decentralized identity wallets depends on collaboration between technology providers, standards organizations, and regulatory bodies. Ensuring that identity wallets comply with legal frameworks such as the General Data Protection Regulation (GDPR) and other data privacy regulations is essential for widespread acceptance. By prioritizing security, interoperability, ease of use, and privacy, identity wallets can become the foundation of a more user-centric digital identity ecosystem.

The Role of Open-Source in Decentralized Identity

Open-source technology plays a fundamental role in the development and adoption of decentralized identity. By providing transparent, auditable, and community-driven solutions, open-source projects ensure that identity systems remain secure, interoperable, and accessible to all users. Decentralized identity, particularly in the context of self-sovereign identity (SSI), relies on trustless systems where users control their credentials without relying on centralized authorities. Open-source principles align perfectly with these objectives, offering transparency, innovation, and global collaboration to build identity solutions that are resistant to monopolization and control by single entities.

One of the most significant benefits of open-source in decentralized identity is transparency. Traditional identity systems are often built on proprietary technologies, which require users to trust that companies are handling their data responsibly. This black-box approach raises concerns about data privacy, security, and hidden vulnerabilities. In contrast, open-source identity frameworks provide full visibility into their codebases, enabling security researchers, developers, and users to audit and verify how identity data is processed and protected. By eliminating the need for blind trust, open-source software fosters a more secure and accountable identity ecosystem.

Security is another critical advantage of open-source decentralized identity solutions. Since decentralized identity depends on cryptographic protocols, secure key management, and verifiable credentials, any flaws in the system could be exploited to compromise user identities. Open-source development enables continuous security auditing and peer review, allowing the global developer community to identify and patch vulnerabilities before they can be exploited by malicious actors. This collaborative approach strengthens the resilience of decentralized identity systems and ensures that they remain robust against evolving cyber threats.

Interoperability is a key challenge in decentralized identity, as various organizations, governments, and institutions develop their own identity frameworks. Without a standardized approach, users may struggle to use their digital identities across different platforms. Open-source projects help address this issue by providing common protocols and standards that enable seamless interoperability. Organizations such as the World Wide Web Consortium (W3C) and the Decentralized Identity Foundation (DIF) promote open standards like decentralized identifiers (DIDs) and verifiable credentials (VCs), ensuring that identity solutions built on different technologies can communicate and verify credentials across networks.

The adoption of open-source decentralized identity solutions reduces vendor lock-in, allowing users and organizations to choose from a variety of implementations without being tied to a single provider. Proprietary identity systems often force users into closed ecosystems, limiting their ability to migrate data, integrate with third-party applications, or modify the software to suit their needs. Open-source identity solutions, on the other hand, empower users with the freedom to select, customize, and deploy identity solutions based on their specific requirements. This flexibility fosters greater innovation and competition in the identity space.

Open-source communities also drive innovation in decentralized identity. Unlike proprietary systems that depend on a single company's development team, open-source projects benefit from contributions from developers, researchers, and experts worldwide. This decentralized approach accelerates technological advancements, leading to new privacy-preserving techniques, improved authentication mechanisms, and more efficient identity verification processes. Emerging technologies such as zero-knowledge proofs (ZKPs), selective disclosure, and privacy-preserving cryptographic protocols have been widely explored within open-source decentralized identity projects.

The role of open-source in identity wallets is particularly important. Identity wallets serve as the interface through which users store, manage, and share verifiable credentials. Open-source wallets provide users with transparency and security, ensuring that their private keys and credentials are not subject to hidden data collection or unauthorized access. Wallets such as the Aries Framework, Trinsic, and MetaMask are examples of open-source projects that enable self-sovereign identity and decentralized authentication. By adopting open-source wallets, users can maintain full control over their digital identities without relying on closed-source applications that may have security or privacy risks.

Another area where open-source plays a vital role is decentralized identity governance. In traditional identity systems, centralized authorities determine identity verification policies, data retention rules, and compliance requirements. Open-source decentralized identity frameworks, on the other hand, enable transparent and community-driven governance models. DAOs (Decentralized Autonomous Organizations) and decentralized governance mechanisms allow identity stakeholders to participate in decision-making processes, ensuring that identity policies are fair, inclusive, and aligned with the needs of users.

The role of open-source is also evident in government-led identity initiatives. Some governments are exploring open-source decentralized identity frameworks to modernize their digital identity infrastructure while maintaining transparency and security. For example, the European Blockchain Services Infrastructure (EBSI) is leveraging open-source identity technologies to enable cross-border identity verification in the European Union. By adopting open standards and community-driven development, governments can create identity solutions that respect user privacy, prevent vendor lock-in, and foster trust among citizens.

Despite the benefits of open-source in decentralized identity, there are challenges that must be addressed. One of the main concerns is sustainability and funding. Many open-source projects rely on volunteer contributions, grant funding, or donations, which can make long-term maintenance difficult. Unlike proprietary solutions backed by commercial business models, open-source projects require collaborative funding mechanisms, such as public grants, enterprise sponsorships, and DAO-based incentives, to ensure continued development and support.

Another challenge is adoption and usability. While open-source projects offer transparency and security, they may sometimes lack the user-friendly interfaces and customer support that proprietary solutions provide. Ensuring that open-source decentralized identity solutions are accessible to non-technical users requires investment in UX/UI design, comprehensive documentation, and community support channels. Projects that prioritize usability, such as Mozilla's open-source initiatives or Linux-based distributions, demonstrate how open-source software can achieve mainstream adoption through intuitive design and user-friendly onboarding processes.

Legal and regulatory compliance is another consideration for open-source decentralized identity solutions. Governments and industries impose strict regulations on identity verification, data protection, and authentication practices. Open-source identity frameworks must align with legal requirements such as the General Data Protection Regulation (GDPR), Know Your Customer (KYC) regulations, and anti-money laundering (AML) laws. Ensuring compliance while maintaining the decentralized and privacy-preserving nature of open-source identity systems requires collaboration between legal experts, developers, and policymakers.

As the decentralized identity ecosystem continues to evolve, open-source will remain a driving force behind innovation, security, and accessibility. By fostering transparency, interoperability, and community-driven development, open-source projects help build a decentralized identity infrastructure that empowers individuals while reducing reliance on centralized authorities. Governments, enterprises, and individual users all stand to benefit from the adoption of open-source identity solutions, ensuring that digital identity remains a fundamental right rather than a product controlled by a select few.

www.ingramcontent.com/pod-product-compliance
Lightning Source LLC
La Vergne TN
LVHW051246050326
832903LV00028B/2596